THE
REVOLUTIONARY WAR
in the
ADIRONDACKS

RAIDS IN THE WILDERNESS

Marie Danielle Annette Williams

THE
History
PRESS

Published by The History Press
Charleston, SC
www.historypress.com

Cover: *Courtesy of Wikimedia Commons.*

First published 2020

Manufactured in the United States

ISBN 9781467142618

Library of Congress Control Number: 2020932105

For Nanny, for always encouraging me to pursue my love of writing and for being the biggest supporter of my love for history.

CONTENTS

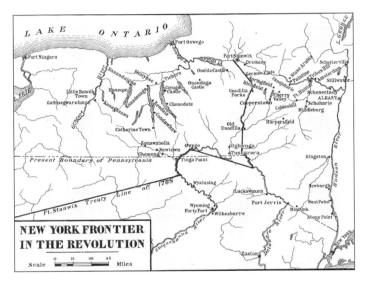

The New York frontier raids in the American Revolution. *F.W. Halsey,*
New York State Archives.

PREFACE

New York played a pivotal role in the American Revolution, one that is often overlooked by the battles and events fought in other would-be states. Over the course of the war, no state would suffer greater losses in both property and population than New York; nearly one-third of all of the major battles and skirmishes of the Revolution took place in New York's borderlands. New York was home to three major military campaigns, and both sides realized the importance of controlling key positions such as New York Harbor, the Hudson Valley and Lake Champlain. However, it was the people above all else who played a role in the Revolution and worked to make it succeed or fail. New York's contribution to the American Revolution should be understood far beyond the importance of just New York City and Saratoga but at the same time should not exclude those areas from the narrative; it should be understood as a multifaceted contribution by Tories and Patriots alike—from different sexes, races and social classes—and viewed as a joint effort of Upstate New York and Downstate New York working together despite the war affecting both areas differently. The American Revolution touched the lives of everyone in the thirteen colonies, and this multifaceted look highlights the fact that the Revolution was a true social revolution as well as a political revolution. This book will examine little-known events of the Revolution in New York that transpired in areas that are often overlooked in terms of the war.

Much of New York State at the time of the American Revolution was frontier wilderness lands sparsely populated by a people who held diverse opinions about the war. Although war truly would not play out in New York north of New York City until mid-1777 with the Saratoga Campaign (although there were smaller events that transpired in 1775), there were other events that would play a role in bringing out beliefs and actions among the people. These events were the raids in the wilderness areas of Upstate and Western New York. The raids would be carried out by the forces of Sir Guy Carleton, his nephew Sir Christopher Carleton, Mohawk war chief Joseph Brant and his cohorts and Edward and Ebenezer Jessup. During the time of the raids, no town was safe. The raids in the wilderness that would begin in the Upstate New York regions with the Carletons and their forces from Canada would spread to other parts of the state as well. The raids in the frontier wilderness areas of Upstate and Western New York are not common topics for discussion or literary narratives and thus are often overlooked as events of the Revolution. For the people who inhabited those areas, however, those raids shaped their perspectives on the war and would shape the war, as people were forced to choose sides, whether they wanted to do so or not.

Many people believe that "history" happened in other places, but the goal of this book is to highlight the importance of these frontier wilderness raids because they show that even small towns tucked away in the mountains and forests played roles just as monumental as the bustling metropolitan areas or the sites of major battles. As an educator, I have had to answer the question of why studying about the past is important when "nothing important" seemed to have happened in the area where my students lived. Many of them were surprised to learn that the town they lived in, where they went to school, where they went with their parents to grocery shop and where they went to hang out at the mall was attacked twice during the American Revolution. I know of only one other historian who chose to focus his research on the British wilderness raids, Canadian historian Gavin K. Watts, who has written numerous accounts of the British raids on New York. Although his work is extremely well researched and can be understood by both those who have and have not studied history, his work lacks the understanding of the raids that those who grew up in the affected areas have. That is where this book comes in. I have spent my entire life, up to this point, in Upstate New York, living my daily life in the Hudson Valley and the Southern Adirondack Mountain regions; the areas' history and stories are what I grew up learning about and are what inspired me to pursue a career in the fields of history and education and are what continue to inspire me years later. This book is the culmination of two years of research about this specific topic.

PREFACE

THERE ARE PERSONAL REASONS for my wanting to write about the British raids on New York's frontier wilderness regions. An ancestor of mine, Robert Dobson, was a lieutenant in the Twentieth Regiment of Foot at the time of the American Revolution. The Twentieth Regiment of Foot saw a handful of engagements during the war for American independence. In April 1776, the regiment was sent from England to Quebec and assisted in the city's relief in May of that year. After the relief of Quebec, the Twentieth Regiment of Foot served under General John Burgoyne during the 1777 Campaign, even fighting and surrendering at the conclusion of the Battle of Saratoga in October 1777. The Twentieth Regiment of Foot was captured and imprisoned with Burgoyne at Saratoga and remained as such until returning to England in 1781. Robert Dobson made his way to Jamaica, where he passed away. Having an ancestor who fought in the American Revolution for the British inspired me, in part, to delve into the actions of the British in New York, particularly after the 1777 Campaign had come to an end.

THE ACT OF RESEARCHING local history is not always an easy task, and the researching, writing, photographing and editing processes were no small feats; however, they were very rewarding, as they showed me that history is my calling. Through the entire process of creating this book, I learned new information about the area I call home and am proud that I get to share this new information with all those who choose to read this book.

ACKNOWLEDGEMENTS

There are so many people who I would like to thank for their encouragements, words of wisdom, assistance and more on this writing journey. I want to thank my family for their love and support and for instilling in me a love of the past and of my home state. I would like to thank my husband's family for their love and support in everything I set out to do. I would like to say a huge thank you to Jeffrey R. Williams for his constant and unconditional love and support in everything I do…and for staying up with me on the nights when I wrote, for making me grilled cheese sandwiches at 1:00 a.m. and for his encouragement to keep writing on the days when I felt like I wanted to give up. There are also so many educators I'd like to thank for encouraging me throughout my journey to become an educator and historian—the history teachers in the Hadley-Luzerne Central School District; the history, political science and adolescent education professors at the College of Saint Rose; and the history professors at Southern New Hampshire University. I would also like to thank everyone at The History Press and Arcadia Publishing for their help putting this book together at all of its different stages.

INTRODUCTION

The people of the Adirondack Mountain region of New York are a unique breed; they are shaped by the actions of those who came long before them and harbor a vast range of ideals and ideologies that were passed down from generation to generation. These are people who understand their past and who have an idea of where they would like to head in the future. If one had to state a time that affected the people of this region deeply in the past, a period that would be correct to choose would be the American Revolution. The people of the Adirondack Mountain region in New York suffered a great deal at the time of America's War of Independence; both those who sided with the Patriot cause and those who sided with the Loyalist cause would raid the small, rural towns of the New York frontier, and on top of that, these were a people who had grown used to the raids carried out by the various Amerindian nations in the vast area. Largely, though, the people of New York were torn about which side to choose for a time; although New York had a sizeable Loyalist population, New York also had a population that was largely apathetic to either side of the war and just wanted to live their lives in relative peace.

The summer of 1777 would bring great changes to the people of Upstate New York, as General John "Gentleman Johnny" Burgoyne led his army through the area, attempting to make his way south from Canada to Albany to capture control of the Hudson River and thus New York in a three-pronged attack to divide the colonies and win the war for Britain, bringing an end to the rebellion. The British, however, were stopped in modern-day Schuylerville, New York, at the Battle of Saratoga. The defeat at Saratoga was just the beginning of the numerous British military actions in the middle colony, as the following year would bring a long series of raids perpetuated by the British on the Patriots in the frontier lands of Upstate New York, which would be a relentless, punishing onslaught until the war's end. Whereas the Americans who chose to side with the Patriot cause were fighting for a freedom they believed they deserved, the British were fighting to keep the British empire whole, even if that meant weaving a path of destruction through the New York frontier.

The scope of the wilderness raids, as far as geography is concerned, is fairly vast, spanning a majority of what would become New York State. The Adirondack Mountain region, the Hudson Valley and the Mohawk Valley saw the most raids. Several smaller settlements in what would become Warren and Saratoga Counties that had raids conducted against them in this time period still exist today, although as previously stated, the raids are not well known in New York history and historiography despite the prominence they played in the war in New York. Some areas in Western New York, particularly modern-day Elmira as well as some former Iroquois settlements, were affected by the raids as well.

Whether the raids directly affected the people of the frontier settlements or indirectly affected the people of the state with fear that they would suffer the same fate as their contemporaries, everyone in the areas north of Westchester County were affected by the British raids in New York from 1778 until 1783.

1

THE SARATOGA CAMPAIGN

The year 1777 was an important one in the American Revolution. Although the war had been raging since 1775, beginning with the Battles of Lexington and Concord in Massachusetts and the Battle of Brooklyn/Long Island in 1776, the people of Upstate New York had been far removed from the events of the war. Whereas people in the Downstate New York areas and other colonies in Colonial America had been forced to choose sides earlier in the conflict, the people of Upstate New York, particularly in the frontier wilderness lands north of Albany, had not yet been exposed to the harsh realities of the war. The summer and autumn of 1777, however, would bring about the Saratoga Campaign, which played an important role in the Revolution as a whole but especially for those who lived in Upstate New York. The Saratoga Campaign was the primary catalyst that triggered multiple wilderness raids in New York as a number of campaigns that affected the people of the state.

The year 1777 would bring about great social changes for the people of Upstate New York, which would greatly affect the second half of the American Revolution. Prior to that year, the people were content to live their everyday lives; although plagued at times by raids from Canada at the hands of the British, the people of the Adirondack Mountains, Mohawk Valley and Hudson Valley regions tended to be either staunch Loyalists or apathetic to either side of the Revolution's cause. While the people of Downstate New York were involved in the war effort for either side, the same revolutionary fervor that had captured the people of New

The fields of the Hudson Valley region of Upstate New York. *Marie D.A. Williams.*

York City had not captured their Upstate counterparts. That is not to say that Patriots were not present in Upstate New York, it was just not to the extent they were present in the Downstate region. One singular event that transpired in the sleepy town of Fort Edward, New York, would change the public perceptions of the Revolution, and of the British and their Native American allies, for centuries.

THE MURDER OF JANE MCCREA

In the summer of 1777, the armies of General Burgoyne and his Iroquois mercenaries were pressing southward from Canada through New York with the goal of dividing the American colonies. Fort Edward was a town that had sprung up around where an abandoned British fort was located, which would come to garrison American troops. It was a crossroads for American, British and Native American troops and would see a lot of military movement between the fort and Rogers Island, where soldiers of both sides were trained for combat service from 1756 and 1781. Prior to the events of

July 1777, however, no military activity in the vicinity of the fort had resulted in bloodshed since 1757, but that would change.

On July 27, 1777, a young woman named Jane McCrea was scalped by a band of Burgoyne's Iroquois mercenaries. Jane was, according to some accounts, heading to her wedding, making her way from the garrison town of Fort Edward to Fort Ticonderoga, when the scalping occurred. To make matters worse, Jane McCrea was a Tory on her way to marry a British soldier, and the indiscriminate killing of a Tory woman by Iroquois mercenaries employed by the British angered and embittered even the staunchest of Loyalist supporters. Jane McCrea's life, prior to her death, was a normal one for that era. Born in New Jersey around 1757, she was the daughter of a Scottish clergyman. She enjoyed reading and was kind and affectionate, religious and described by friends as being uncommonly beautiful.

The murder of the young Loyalist bride Jane McCrea would cause controversies between both sides of the Revolutionary conflict and on both sides of the Atlantic. American leader General Gates wrote Burgoyne a scathing letter, blaming him for the tragedy that befell Jane McCrea. Even Sir Edmund Burke, a Whig member of British Parliament, would use the tragedy to rail against the policies of the Crown, particularly when it came to allowing generals and Native mercenaries to run amuck.

The murder of this young woman would inspire New Yorkers to take up the Patriot cause and grow the ranks of the Continental army at a time when desertion was otherwise high. Jane McCrea's murder would yield major social effects in Upstate New York. The local population who were Loyalist or otherwise apathetic to the Revolution as a whole would join the cause and become fervent supporters of American patriotism in the wake of Native American raids and indiscriminate murders. To them, the Loyalist cause was not one to support.

American soldiers lined up for battle. *Marie D.A. Williams.*

The events after the murder of Jane McCrea would become a part of the famed Saratoga Campaign, which pegged the British and Americans against one another in numerous locations in the Hudson Valley region of Upstate New York. The military campaign, along with small raids perpetuated by the British and its Iroquois allies, was meant to cripple the American forces as a last-ditch effort to capture New York, a middle colony, for the British.

THE SARATOGA CAMPAIGN

If a singular event, or a series of events, could be attributed to the frontier raids perpetuated by the British, it would be the Saratoga Campaign, which occurred in the summer and autumn of 1777. The Saratoga Campaign was one of three major military campaigns that took place in New York at the time of the American Revolution. Consisting of a series of battles in Upstate New York at Fort Anne, Stanwix, Oriskany, Walloomsac (ten miles east of Bennington) and Saratoga, the Saratoga Campaign would have major social effects on the people living in those areas. Although the Saratoga Campaign was a military campaign, in order to fully grasp the events that occured during the campaign, one must study and understand the human aspect of the war. To do this, this section describes the battles of the Saratoga Campaign to a minor extent and discusses the response the battles received from those who lived in the areas affected by the battles and how the battles would affect their lives during the Revolution. As a sum of the experiences of the Saratoga Campaign, the campaign was important, as it would bring on the first major American victory of the war and a turning point of the Revolution. The American victory at the conclusion of the Saratoga Campaign would usher in an alliance between France and the American forces; later in the course of the war, Spain and the Netherlands would ally with the Americans as well. The victory at the conclusion of the Saratoga Campaign showed the true strength that the American forces possessed; while many were untrained in the ways of military actions, they were passionate for their cause, and that was a major driving force behind the American victory at Saratoga and in later battles of the war as well.

General Burgoyne's army began making its way south from St. Johns, Canada, in early June 1777. As the British soldiers made their move south through the wilderness of New York, they encountered the Americans at Fort Ticonderoga, where the British retook the fort from the Americans. As

An officer discusses horse care on the battlefield. *Marie D.A. Williams.*

American soldiers relax in the autumn afternoon sun. *Marie D.A. Williams.*

the Americans retreated through Skenesborough, they would fell trees, burn bridges and block the roads that the British would take as they continued to make their way south, attempting to reach the Hudson River for a smoother journey south. On July 30, 1777, Burgoyne's army reached the ruins of the defunct Fort Edward.

The journey to the fort was rife with complications. The journey took longer than predicted, and Burgoyne's army was short on supplies. Also, as they passed through the rural frontier lands of Upstate New York, Burgoyne hoped to attract more Loyalists to join his ranks, but the number of Loyalists he had expected to acquire did not come. As Burgoyne's ranks moved south from Canada, another force, under the British brevet brigadier general Barrimore "Barry" St. Leger, moved from Fort Oswego on Lake Ontario through the Mohawk Valley, where he was supposed to meet Burgoyne at Albany. A third army, led by General Henry Clinton, was supposed to move north from New York City to Albany. As the three British armies converged on Albany, the American colonies would be severed and a victory by the British over the American would be had. This British plan would not come

Cannon overlooking the Hudson Valley. *Marie D.A. Williams.*

to pass, as Burgoyne refused to garrison his men at either Fort Ticonderoga or Fort Edward when his supplies were running low, and chose to move on with the three-pronged strategy to capture New York.

THE BATTLE OF FORT ANNE

As Burgoyne's army made its way from Canada to Albany, it would encounter the American forces in numerous battles along that journey, ending with the Battles of Saratoga, two battles in modern-day Stillwater, New York, located about ten miles away from the village of Saratoga. One of the earliest of these encounters was the Battle of Fort Anne, which took place in modern-day Fort Ann, New York. (The *E* was dropped in later years.) Long seen as a minor skirmish, the Battle of Fort Anne was recognized as the Americans' first stand against Burgoyne's army, and the social implications signaled the change of American morale and a depletion of Burgoyne's forces as they continued to make their way south to Albany. These led to an increased feeling of patriotism and a growth in participation of New Yorkers on the side of the Americans, that benefited the American forces for the duration of the war.

The Battle of Fort Anne occurred on July 8, 1777, as the Americans were making their retreat from Fort Ticonderoga to Skenesborough, where they would continue on to Fort Edward. Burgoyne's forces met with the retreating Americans and opened fire on them. In a retreat from Skenesborough, the Americans set fire to the area, which worked to slow the British advance, and made their way to Fort Anne. Captain James Gray, who was a captain in a New Hampshire regiment, recorded the events of the battle on the back of a roster for his regiment:

> *Monday, 7th, — Got into Fort Anne at 6 in ye morning; everything in the utmost confusion; nothing to eat. General Philip Schuyler had sent 400 New York militia under Henry Van Rensselaer to Fort Anne to meet those retreating from Ticonderoga. At 11 o'clock A.M. (the same morning I arrived) was ordered to take the Command of a party upon a scout and marched with 150 men besides 17 Rangers; had not marched from Garrison into the woods more than half a mile, after detaching my front, Rear and flanking Guards, when we met with a party of Regulars and gave them fire, which was Returned by the enemy, who then gave back. I then pursued them with close fire till they betook themselves to the top of a*

A soldier's lean-to tent and belongings. *Marie D.A. Williams.*

mountain. At the foot of this mountain we posted our selves and continued our fire until 6 P.M., when a reinforcement of 150 more joined me; but night approaching obliged me to return with my party to Garrison, after finding one of my party killed and 3 wounded, and three of the enemy killed by our first fire. Tuesday Morning, 8th,—Myself, with Capt. Hutchins, with the same number of men, marched to the aforesaid mountain and attacked the enemy very warmly. The engagement lasted about 2 hours, at which time the Commander of yo Garrison sent Colo. Ransleur [Colonel Van Rensselaer] *with a small party of militia to reinforce us. We then advanced up the hill, where we found the enemy's surgeon dressing a Capts Leg. Those, with two of their wounded soldiers, we took and sent in, and a number of our own people, men & women, who were the day before cut off by the enemy, we retook. At last, finding out ammunition gone and none to be had in Garrison, ordered off my wounded and some of the dead, and formed a retreat. Much fatigued when I returned and found no refreshments, neither meat or drink; immediately a Council was called and the prisoners who were retaken brot upon examination, who gave information that an express just arrived before we made this second attack and gave the enemy intelligence that a reinforcement of 2,000, with Indians, were near at hand to join them, at which time they were to make a general attack upon us. It was then determined upon to retreat to fort Edward, after setting fire the Garrison. Accordingly, the wounded were sent off, except one, who was one of my own Company; him the Surgeon thot proper not to order off, that he would soon expire, or that if he was likely to live, the enemy, when they took possession, would take care of him. This I knew not of till we were ordered to march, at which time I turned back alone (my Company being gone) to the rear of the Army, where I found him. I then picked up a tent & fastened it between two poles, laid him upon it, and hired four soldiers to carry him. I took their four guns with my own and carried them to fort Edward; this was about 3 o'clock P.M.; rained very hard; distance from Fort Anne to Fort Edward, 14 miles; arrived at Fort Edward at 10 in the Evening; no Barracks nor Tents to go into; therefore laid down in the rain and slept upon the ground; the fatigue of this day I believe I shall always remember. Colo Ransleur, wounded; Capt Weare, wounded; Ensign Walcutt, killed; Isaac Davis, a sergeant in my company, killed. Our loss in the two skirmishes about 15; the Enemy's unknown.*

Civilian camp followers go about their daily lives at the Freeman Farmhouse at the Saratoga National Battlefield Park. *Marie D.A. Williams.*

The firsthand account of the events at the Battle of Fort Anne highlights what the soldiers endured over the course of the battle and the condition they were in as the surviving soldiers made their way to garrison at Fort Edward. However, the soldiers would later find themselves at one of the most pivotal battles of the Revolution in the fall of 1777, at Saratoga.

THE SIEGE OF FORT STANWIX AND THE BATTLE OF ORISKANY

As Burgoyne's army continued its way south, the British forces under St. Leger were moving across the state as well, and in August, the British under St. Leger would besiege an American fort, Fort Stanwix, near modern-day Rome, New York.

The forces of Brevet Brigadier General Barry St. Leger would come on Fort Schuyler, more famously known as Fort Stanwix, in early August 1777. Fort Stanwix was situated in the upper Mohawk River Valley and guarded a critical area of the Mohawk River; however, the British under St. Leger were

Soldiers' tents on the battlefield's encampment. *Marie D.A. Williams.*

unable to take the fort in a head-on attack, so the forces of St. Leger besieged the fort to force a surrender. The British had attempted to cut off a supply line from arriving to the fort but were unsuccessful.

St. Leger demanded the surrender of the fort, but the American forces, under Colonel Peter Gansevoort and Lieutenant Colonel Marinus Willett, refused to surrender the fort. St. Leger's army surrounded the fort and fired on it with muskets and rifles. They were unable to access thier heavy artillery, which was floated down the Wood Creek and stuck on the boats due to the Americans felling trees and burning bridges in the area. The British besieged the fort for around twenty days before aid came to them. During that period, soldiers recorded what they experienced in their journals. One of those soldiers was Ensign William Colbreth of the Third New York Regiment. In his journal, he stated:

> *Augt. 12th. The Enemy kept out of sight all day and no firing from them till Noon when they gave us some Shott and Shells, without doing any damage. We Imagined the Enemy drew their Forces in the Day Time between us and Orisko, as we have not seen them so plenty these two or three Days as we are used to do. Neither do they trouble us all night, which gave our Troops an Opportunity of Resting. Augt. 13th. The Enemy were very peaceable all days towards Night when they Cannonaded and Bombarded for two Hours, during which Time a Shell broke a Soldier's Leg belonging to Colonel Millen's Detachment.*

As the days of the siege drew on, Ensign Colbreth continued to record the actions and inactions of the soldiers on both sides of the siege; in several of his journal entries, he described the wounds the soldiers endured and any deaths that occurred due to soldiers being wounded in the siege, and he also described several occurrences in which American soldiers deserted their posts.

Beginning on August 6, 1777, the Battle of Oriskany took place in the vicinity of Fort Stanwix. The Battle of Oriskany would be one of the bloodiest battles in the American Revolution and was a result of Brigadier General Nickolas Herkimer and his men coming to the relief of the besieged Fort Stanwix. The Tryon County militia and their Oneida allies were ambushed by the Mohawk allies of the British under the command of Chief Joseph Brant as they were making their way to Fort Stanwix. In the ambush, Herkimer was injured in the leg but would continue to lead his men as he sat under a tree, directing them to work in teams of two, so while one

Camp followers discuss what life in the encampment was like with park visitors at the Saratoga National Battlefield Park. *Marie D.A. Williams.*

soldier reloaded his musket or rifle, he was covered. Despite his best efforts, the Americans would be forced off the field. However, the Tryon County militia under Herkimer was able to assist the men stationed at Fort Stanwix. What seemed like an initial victory for St. Leger at the defeat of Herkimer's men would prove to be a temporary loss as his men wavered, unable to take the fort or force a surrender, and St. Leger would give up the fight for Fort Stanwix on hearing word of Benedict Arnold and his men moving to assist Herkimer and the besieged fort.

Under Lieutenant Colonel Marius Willett, raids were carried out on St. Leger's camps as they retreated. In one of the raids, a mailbag that was supposed to have been delivered to Fort Stanwix but was confiscated by St. Leger's men was returned to the fort. In the mailbag was a letter to Colonel Peter Gansevoort written by the woman he loved. When his men asked if he had plans to marry his love, he responded that if they could get through battle alive, he would marry, and on January 12, 1778, Colonel Peter Gansevoort married Catherine "Katie" Van Schaik. As for Herkimer, he would die from the wounds he sustained in battle on August 16, 1777,

Mohawk war chief Joseph Brandt. *Wikimedia Commons.*

but his legacy would live on in a song that was written shortly after the Battle of Oriskany, titled "General Herkimer's Battle," written by an author under the penname "Juvinus."

The social implications of the Battle of Oriskany were great. Due to the huge loss of life of the local militiamen as well as the felling of trees, the burning of bridges and both sides of the conflict burning down structures

A British cannon overlooking the battlefield. *Marie D.A. Williams.*

in which the enemy could find cover, the area was in devastation. Families in the area were prompted to leave due to the war and raids carried out by Chief Joseph Brant, which would last through the end of the Revolution. The area was colloquially known as the "bread basket" of the state, as that was where the most farms, specifically for grains such as wheat, rye, oats and barley, were located, and the grains that were produced on those farms were for the benefit of the families who ran them but also for the armies and citizens of the state. The lack of grain farming in the area as the war went on meant that the armies were not getting the necessary rations they required at a time when supplies, especially for the American forces, were already very low.

THE BATTLE OF BENNINGTON

The Battle of Oriskany would lead to continued fighting in the area, and the Saratoga Campaign would grow. Soon, another battle would be underway in Walloomsac, New York, about ten miles away from Bennington, Vermont.

The Battle of Bennington, in the town of Walloomsac, New York, was the last battle before the Americans and the British would face off at the pivotal Battle of Saratoga. Taking place between August 14 and August 16, 1777, the Battle of Bennington would bring a small American victory, with Major General John Stark's American forces defeating two detachments of General John Burgoyne's advancing army.

Due to previous military engagements, the British found themselves low on supplies and heard that there were stores in Bennington. The Americans, under Stark, attacked the British from multiple angles as they encamped near the Walloomsac River. Another detachment of Burgoyne's troops was sent to fight to help their outnumbered comrades. As the Americans were beaten back by the British, an American force, Colonel Seth Warner and his Green Mountain Boys, came to Stark's aid. The Americans were able to overpower the British, and the British retreated in an unorganized manner.

Many of Burgoyne's men who fought at the Battle of Bennington were from his Iroquois forces, and Bennington would mark the beginning of the end for many of Burgoyne's men. With the devastating loss sustained by the British at the Battle of Bennington, the British, German and Iroquois

Camp followers have an amusing discussion. *Marie D.A. Williams.*

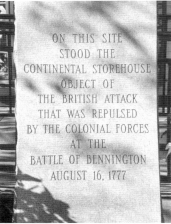

Left: Bennington Monument. *Library of Congress*.

Above: A plaque commemorating the Battle of Bennington. *Marie D.A. Williams*.

desertion rates would rise. This loss of able-bodied soldiers would have a devastating effect on the British army, as it would play a role in the British defeat at the Battle of Saratoga. After the Battle of Bennington, the Patriot forces would engage in the torture and murder of captured British soldiers. The treatment the British captives faced at the hands of the Americans would show that the rules of engagement that existed at the time for battles and war would no longer be regarded.

THE BATTLES OF SARATOGA

The American victory at Bennington would further halt the British advance; this would allow the Americans who had already reached the site of the Battle of Saratoga time to dig into the earth, creating breastworks and other earthworks to protect themselves on the terrain. In September 1777, the first of the engagements at Saratoga, the Battle of Freeman's Farm, would occur, with the second engagement, the Battle of Bemis Heights, in October 1777. Burgoyne's plan for the Saratoga Campaign, once again, was to head to Albany and then link up with the British troops who were garrisoned in New

A leather worker shows off his craft. *Marie D.A. Williams.*

York City, where they would cut the American colonies in two. The area that would become the Saratoga Battlefield was chosen by the American leader General Horatio Gates to stop the British advance toward Albany. The land was owned by the Bemis and Freeman families, both Loyalists, as well as the Neilson family, who served in the American army.

On September 19, 1777, the British under Burgoyne and the Americans under Gates engaged in battle. The Americans had established themselves at Bemis Heights, which would become an important defensive position along the Hudson River. The Americans had fortifications on the floodplain and cannons on the Heights, and Burgoyne's forces had been using the Hudson River to transport supplies; the American defenses on the Heights were unavoidable. Learning of the American defenses at Bemis Heights, Burgoyne moved his army inland to avoid the danger but collided with part of General Gates's army near the abandoned Freeman Farm. During the fighting on September 19, the British were unable to gain any ground or maintain any momentum. Later in the day, German auxiliary troops under Baron von Riedesel turned the tide of the battle for the British forces. The baron's wife, the Baroness von Riedesel, kept a journal throughout the course of the war and would write about the Battle of Freeman's Farm; in it, she wrote that she feared for her husband's life when she realized he was part of the battle. The British had two thousand women and servants who attended to the Battles of Saratoga with them, and the existence of the baroness's diary is an astonishing source that gives historians a look into the past at what the women had to endure in the camp, as well as the personal thoughts of the baroness on the strategic Battle of Saratoga.

The British had suffered heavy casualties at this first battle, and with supplies running dangerously low, Burgoyne made the conscious decision to wait for reinforcements and supplies from General Henry Clinton in New York City. As September turned to October, Burgoyne realized that Clinton's reinforcements from New York City would not be making their way to the Stillwater/Saratoga area. On October 7, Burgoyne tried to make another attack at the Battle of Bemis Heights. Benedict Arnold, who had been ordered to stay in his tent by General Gates after an argument, disobeyed the commanding officer and rallied his troops at Balcarres Redoubt, where he sustained an injury to his leg. The British were driven back, and under the cover of darkness, they stacked their arms and retreated into Saratoga. On October 17, 1777, General John Burgoyne surrendered to General Horatio Gates, putting an end to the Battles of Saratoga and the British strategy to take the Hudson River and divide the colonies—for a time.

Despite the bravery of Arnold's actions, historians continue to argue the validity of what happened on the Balcarres Redoubt in regard to his presence. Historian George Bancroft and founder of the Sons of the Revolution John Austin Stevens questioned whether Arnold was truly on the field during the Battle of Saratoga, particularly the Battle of Freeman's Farm on September 19. Bancroft was met with scrutiny by Isaac N. Arnold, famous for being Abraham Lincoln's biographer, who would use letters written by Benedict Arnold's aide to describe the actions at the first Battle of Saratoga, refuting the claims made by Stevens and Bancroft. In a piece titled "Benedict Arnold at Saratoga: Reply to John Austin Stevens, and New Evidence of Mr. Bancroft's Error," published by Isaac N. Arnold in 1880, he describes the actions he took to be able to refute the claims made by Stevens and Bancroft. Using the letter written by Benedict Arnold's aide, Isaac Arnold stated that Benedict Arnold had to have been on the field the day of September 19, 1777, as Colonel Daniel Morgan and his men would receive orders from Benedict Arnold during the battle. Why would respectable historians such as Bancroft report that Benedict Arnold was not on the field on the day of September 19, 1777, when there is evidence written by his aide that suggests otherwise? One answer could be that Benedict Arnold would later betray the American cause, so it is a sort of revisionism. Arnold has a monument dedicated to him at Saratoga Battlefield, the famous boot monument, but due to his betrayal, the monument does not bear his name.

THE BATTLE OF SARATOGA had a major social impact on the course of the war. As a consequence, for their siding with the British, the Bemis and Freeman families would lose their property at the war's end and would go to Canada, as would many Loyalists whose property was dispossessed. The act of dispossessing Loyalists from their properties would continue over the course of the war, and at its end, and families would lose huge tracts of land and other property as a consequence of being on the wrong side during the war. Other social effects include the publication of private diaries, which would provide an accurate portrayal of the events of the Revolution and the people who were involved in it.

One such diary to be published at the end of the war was that of the Baroness von Riedesel, whose writing would provide historians with a look into the past that was unique to a woman of standing who sided with the British during the war. Her diary told not only of the events at the Battle of Saratoga but also the British retreat from Saratoga to Boston, where the Riedesels would live for a year before moving to the South, where the military action at the time was light and the baroness and her children would be out of harm's way. Another major result of the Battle of Saratoga was the act of the rules of engagement no longer being applicable; Colonel Morgan's group of Kentucky Riflemen were known for using guerrilla tactics during the battle—they hid in the trees around the battlefield and would shoot at the British commanding officers, leaving the soldiers without leaders. This was an act that was frowned on in previous battles and in previous wars, but it was a tactic that would prove useful to the Americans.

The Battle of Saratoga, and the Saratoga Campaign as a whole, would be a turning point in the Revolution. The success of the American forces in these battles would drive the British forces from battling the Americans in New York for a time and would show the world that the colonies, although not educated in the ways of war to the extent of the British military, could hold their own and be successful. From the victory at the Battle of Saratoga came agreements between the French and the Americans and the Dutch and the Americans, who each pledged to provide the fledgling army with

Camp followers mend the clothes of soldiers. *Marie D.A. Williams.*

Camp followers relax on the porch of the Freeman Farmhouse. *Marie D.A. Williams.*

men, ships and money to fight the remainder of the war. This would change the tide of the war in the Americans' favor.

With the British unable to take New York and split the colonies in half as they intended, the British would leave New York for a time and would focus their energy on battles elsewhere. However, beginning in 1778, the British would return to New York and conduct raids in its frontier regions. The Old World style of fighting that the British had adapted in the first half of the Revolution would be useless in the frontier raids, so they enlisted the help of Loyalists from the regions they planned to attack, as well as from the local Iroquois nations who chose to ally themselves with the Crown, as the perpetrators for these raids. These frontier raids, a last-ditch effort to weaken New York so the rest of the colonies would fall, played a major role in the Revolution in New York, despite being little known among the current population.

2

THE KING'S MEN

The British army in North America was extremely well organized. New York had a sizeable Loyalist population, and those Loyalist men were eager to join the military and take up arms for King George III. Although the exact number of Loyalists who joined the ranks remains unknown, the different detachments that were present in Upstate New York, their establishment and the exact role they played are known. In the Champlain, Hudson and Mohawk Valleys, the Loyalist men who joined the ranks were as passionate for their cause as the men they fought against. Many of these men resided in the areas they would take part in raids against and would fight with the same fury to protect their families, land and other properties. These men, the king's men, were organized in several regiments and detachments across the state of New York. Although the Loyalists lost the war and America gained its independence from Great Britain, Canada grew because of these men.

BUTLER'S RANGERS

Butler's Rangers made famous the irregular warfare on New York's frontier. Colonel John Butler and his son Walter raided the New York/Pennsylvania border established after the conclusion of the Battle of Oriskany in 1777. Both Butlers were involved in raids—John was involved in the Battle of

The British flag waving in the breeze. *Marie D.A. Williams.*

Wyoming Valley in Pennsylvania, which has become known as the Wyoming Valley Massacre, and both Butlers participated in the raid on Cherry Valley in New York, which would become known as the Cherry Valley Massacre. The irregular warfare of the raids used by the British and the particular hit-and-run style of warfare exemplified by the Butlers worked to draw off American troops and either destroy their supplies or successfully capture those supplies for use by the British military. The raids perpetrated by Butler's Rangers, along with the detachments led by John Johnson and Joseph Brant, were so destructive that the Americans launched the Sullivan/Clinton Campaign in 1779 to attempt to put an end to the raids. Butler's Rangers were in operation until 1784, after the conclusion of the American Revolution. As a result of their services no longer being needed in the New York frontier, many of the members of the disbanded regiment settled on the Niagara frontier and established their own communities and towns, such as St. Catharines in Ontario.

Prior to the outbreak of the American Revolution, John Butler had been a successful farmer in the Mohawk River Valley near Fort Hunter, which is modern-day Fonda, New York. At the time, he was ranked as a lieutenant colonel in New York's colonial militia and he had been appointed to the position of deputy superintendent of the British Indian Department.

In 1775, many of New York's Loyalists had fled to Canada to escape arrest for their chosen political side. Due to this, in June 1775, Colonel Guy Johnson, son of Sir William Johnson and brother of Sir John Johnson, moved the headquarters of the British Indian Department to Montreal. John Butler moved as well, and in November of that year, he was posted to Fort Niagara with the mission of maintaining neutrality among the Iroquois Six Nations according to British policy, and in this, he was moderately successful.

In 1777, the British had realized that the Americans speaking of freedom from British rule might have an effect on the Six Nations, particularly fearing that the Iroquois might side with the Americans, as the Oneida had already done. Due to this fear that the Natives might side with the Americans, the British sent instructions to Sir Guy Carleton, the governor of Quebec and its commander-in-chief, to engage the Six Nations in an expedition led by Lieutenant Colonel Barry St. Leger. This expedition was part of a grand strategy to secure New York, as had been attempted the previous year by General and Admiral Howe at the Battle of Long Island. St. Leger commanded the right wing of an invasion of Upstate New York, entering New York at Oswego and moving down the Mohawk River to Albany, where the plan was to meet up with General John Burgoyne's army. Together, this combined army would make contact with a third army moving north from New York City.

John Butler gathered a large force of Native Americans at Oswego in August 1777 to fight alongside the forces of St. Leger. This event, the siege of Fort Stanwix, would see Butler rise to the occasion as a British officer. At this siege, St. Leger was unable to capture Fort Stanwix. The Americans gathered on the Mohawk River and established a column of six hundred men. Sir John Johnson made to attack the column, supported by Butler and the Natives under his command. The siege of Fort Stanwix was successful in all, allowing the British to decimate the Americans; however, the Natives were not impressed with the slow-going process and drifted away from the British, forcing St. Leger to abandon his leg of the expedition to capture New York.

Governor Sir Guy Carleton was so impressed with Butler's success commanding the Natives in his ranks that he authorized Butler to raise a corps of rangers to serve with him in New York's frontier. Butler's Corps of Rangers, known more commonly as Butler's Rangers, was officially established on September 15, 1777. Recruiting soldiers for the corps was slow at first, but by mid-December the first company was mustered.

In the spring of 1778, Butler and his rangers moved into the New York frontier, where they held conferences with the Native peoples of the area and dispatched small raiding parties against the few American fortifications. By late June of that year, Butler's Rangers had a fighting force of two hundred rangers and three hundred Indian warriors, and they moved against Wyoming, Pennsylvania (modern-day Wilkes-Barre). The small fortifications in the area surrendered quickly to Butler's Rangers, but an American force held out in Forty Fort. Butler was able to lure the Americans out of the fort by feigning retreat, and the rangers fought fiercely against the American forces and completely defeated them. After what would become known as the Wyoming Valley Massacre, Butler's Rangers returned to New York and would conduct raids against the towns and fortifications in the New York frontier.

One event shortly after the Wyoming Valley Massacre would leave a stain on the history of Butler's Rangers. On November 10, 1778, Butler's son Walter Butler led a raid alongside Joseph Brant into Cherry Valley, New York. The British raid on Cherry Valley was a punishing assault; the

Scottish soldiers relaxing in the autumn sun. *Marie D.A. Williams.*

American troops hid in the fort for refuge, which left the civilians to fend for themselves against the onslaught. The British were indiscriminate in their killings at the time of the raid, and Joseph Brant himself was distraught when he realized that the British soldiers and the Mohawk warriors under his command had wounded and killed Loyalists he knew personally. What was worse, the Mohawk warriors discovered that there were American soldiers who had surrendered in a previous encounter and had been on parole. As a response to this discovery, the warriors ravaged the village and killed men, women and children, regardless of their side of the war.

John Butler and his rangers would continue to encounter American troops. In 1779, the Americans launched the Sullivan/Clinton Expedition and engaged the British and their Amerindian allies at Newtown in modern-day Elmira, New York. The Sullivan/Clinton Expedition was launched by General George Washington as a response to the British raids on the frontier. As many of the perpetrators of these raids were Amerindian, the expedition sought to quell the raids by hitting the British where it would hurt the most. The Americans destroyed almost every village they entered, and at Newtown, Butler and his rangers made an attempt to defeat the Americans, but Butler's assault failed, as his position was threatened by flanking forces. Butler ordered a retreat but would attempt to spring a trap on the Americans by engaging them at the head of Lake Conesus. Butler was unsuccessful and was forced to withdraw, but Sullivan, who was making toward the withdrawing British, had stretched his supplies to the breaking point and was forced to turn back from his pursuit of the British.

Butler's Rangers conducted a number of raids against the New York frontier throughout 1780. In the fall of that year, Sir John Johnson was ordered to begin his own series of raids into the Mohawk Valley region of Upstate New York, setting off from Oswego, and Butler's Rangers were ordered to join Johnson's raiders. Johnson's raid, with backup from Butler's Rangers, was extremely successful, and the destruction carried out by the British would have long-lasting consequences for the people and the land of New York.

Butler's Rangers would see action in the western territories, particularly in Detroit, Michigan, and Sandusky, Ohio. In one of these western expeditions, Walter Butler was killed in action. Butler's Rangers returned to the Niagara area toward the end of the Revolution. In June 1784, the company was reduced in strength and was mustered out of action.

THE KING'S ROYAL REGIMENT OF NEW YORK

In June 1776, after his escape to avoid arrest by the Americans for his Loyalist leanings, Sir John Johnson raised the King's Royal Regiment of New York, known colloquially as Johnson's Greens. Johnson's Greens were refugees from the Mohawk and Schoharie Valleys, many also having fled to Canada to escape arrest by the Americans, which was beneficial for the British, as they could successfully carry out raids in those Upstate areas and ensure that no farmhouse—no matter how remote—was left unmolested. Johnson's Greens would eventually form two battalions and would use Oswego as its jumping-off point for the raids it led. Johnson, like John Butler, was known for his raids throughout his former homeland of Upstate New York and would also cut his teeth on the act of frontier warfare at the Battle of Oriskany during Burgoyne's 1777 Campaign. Johnson's Greens would become known, and feared, for the savagery they displayed on their former neighbors and on any other enemies they encountered.

Sir John Johnson had inherited his father's title. Sir William Johnson was a fur trader who immigrated to the Mohawk Valley in the earlier eighteenth century and was known for establishing relations with the Six Nations on behalf of Great Britain at the time of the pivotal Seven Years' War. This title and his loyalties to Great Britain came with a price—the Americans had threatened John Johnson and others with arrest and had begun destroying Loyalist-owned businesses, mills and homes. Johnson even had to go so far as to fortify his home and arm both the white tenants on the Johnson patent and Iroquois allies, who also suffered threats from American rebels. Fearing for their lives, many Loyalists in New York fled to Canada, like the men in Butler's Rangers, as well as Johnson and many others.

Around the time many New York Loyalists fled to Canada, the Americans' Continental Congress raised an army and sought to invade Canada. At Quebec, the American forces led by General Montgomery, among others, were defeated in the winter of 1775–76. Although the American invasion of Canada failed, colonials were causing distress in the Mohawk Valley and making moves against Johnson's property. Johnson had been warned of the Americans' movements—they had disarmed his tenants and were planning to arrest him. With his tenants defenseless, and unable to launch a defense of his home himself, Johnson had no choice but to escape to Canada. With two hundred followers and an unknown number of Mohawk warriors, Johnson made his way to Canada. The escape was long and arduous, as the band had to make its way through the wintry Adirondack Mountains with few

British superintendent of Indian Affairs Sir William Johnson. *Wikimedia Commons.*

weapons and provisions, but in the spring of 1776, Johnson's band, weakened and starving, arrived in Montreal. One of the first things Johnson did after arriving in Montreal was seek out the governor for approval to raise his own regiment, which he was granted by Governor Guy Carleton and began recruiting shortly thereafter. The King's Royal Regiment of New York, Johnson's Greens, comprised primarily those who had followed Johnson to Canada, but many others volunteered for the regiment as well.

The first major campaign that Johnson's Greens participated in was the Battle of Oriskany, a major battle of Burgoyne's 1777 Campaign. While a major British fighting force moved south from Canada to invade New York, another force moved east from Oswego with the intent of overpowering the Mohawk Valley. Both of these forces moved as far as the American garrison at Fort Stanwix, where they would make their attack. An American militia of the valley moved to relieve the besieged fort. The British were informed by this movement, and Johnson's Greens, the Indian Department Rangers, Amerindians from the Six Nations and Joseph Brant's forces laid in wait in Oriskany. This ambush devastated the Americans, and General Herkimer was fatally wounded in the assault. The Battle of Oriskany was not just a major victory for the British, but it was also a victory for Johnson's Greens, which endured its first military encounter.

Throughout the remainder of the Revolution, Johnson's Greens continued to prove its military strength with a number of raids in the soldiers' former communities in the Mohawk and Schoharie Valleys. With these raids, Johnson was able to achieve several objectives: his men rescued Loyalists who were forced to endure raids by the Americans; they destroyed local farms, homes and livestock and harvests intended to feed the American military; and the continual raids by Johnson's Greens lowered the morale of the American military and those with Patriot leanings in the Mohawk and Schoharie Valleys. A major raiding campaign Johnson and his Greens were involved in was called the Burning of the Valleys—a 1780 raiding campaign perpetrated by Sir John Johnson and Joseph Brant with the goal of utter destruction. The Burning of the Valleys campaign was so effective on the New York frontier that long after the American Revolution had concluded, much of the land of the Mohawk Valley was useless; however, with the scratch of a pen, the land that the Loyalists had fought so hard to maintain control of—the land many of them had called home—had been granted to the new United States of America.

BRANT'S VOLUNTEERS

During the American Revolution, the Six Nations of the Iroquois chose sides, with the hope that the respective side each nation chose would benefit them with the outcome of the war. One man, Mohawk war chief Joseph Brant, played a monumental role during the war, leading raiding parties against the American forces in Upstate and Western New York and being a leading perpetrator of the Burning of the Valleys. Brant had close ties to the Johnson family, as he acted as an interpreter for Sir William Johnson, and his sister Molly Brant was Sir William Johnson's mistress. Due to these familial connections, Joseph Brant unsurprisingly sided with the Loyalist cause, as did many of the Mohawk Amerindians.

Throughout the war, Brant led various raids through the Mohawk Valley region and beyond with an irregular fighting force of both whites and Amerindians beginning in 1777. Initially, Brant paid out of his own pocket to ensure his volunteer troops were fed, equipped and outfitted and paid, but over time, Sir Frederick Haldimand, a British Canadian governor, authorized the outfitting and provisioning of Brant's Volunteers. However, Brant's Volunteers was not recognized as a military unit and was not on the British army payroll, so many members of the volunteers would transfer to either Butler's Rangers or Johnson's Greens to be paid for their military service under the Crown. Brant's Volunteers had a long history throughout the Revolution, and his men would be involved in countless raids throughout New York.

Joseph Brant had extensive knowledge of the British way of life in North America, and it was this knowledge and his experiences as a Mohawk that would make him align himself with the Crown at the time of the American Revolution. As a boy, Brant received an education from Sir William Johnson, the head of the British Six Nations Department of Indian Affairs and his sister's husband. Through the education he gained under the tutelage of Johnson, Brant learned about Mohawk-British relations and how the British

Soldiers and a camp follower mingle. *Marie D.A. Williams.*

worked to maintain relationships with their Amerindian allies. Receiving this behind-the-scenes look into life in colonial Upstate New York encouraged Brant to participate in the Seven Years' War at the Battle of Lake George in 1755, where he would fight honorably and earn his status as a warrior. Brant was also active militarily during Pontiac's Rebellion in 1763. Brant was not just a military man, but he also worked with Daniel Claus, Sir William Johnson's son-in-law, to translate the *Anglican Book of Common Prayer* into the Mohawk language, and when Guy Johnson took on the position of superintendent of Indian Affairs, Brant took on the position of his secretary.

Brant left the Mohawk Valley in 1775, following the death of Sir William Johnson, and traveled with Guy Johnson to Montreal, where he participated in the defense of the city from an American attack in October of that year. Following that, Brant sailed to England and had a meeting with King George III and other government officials to air the grievances of the Mohawk people. This meeting went well, and Brant was well received in England, and it was this meeting and his reception in England that cemented his feelings of loyalty to the Crown and to its cause of maintaining its colonies in North America. Once he returned to America, Brant set about on raising the King's

Standard, which would be known colloquially as Brant's Volunteers. Joseph Brant raised his volunteer corps in 1777; although Brant was active through the entirety of the American War for Independence, this first fighting force of his was active for only two years, being mustered out of action in 1779. Brant's Volunteers was few in number, with only an estimated one hundred men in their ranks. The volunteers were of mixed company, with around twenty of those men being members of the Six Nations and the remaining eighty or so men being white. Brant's Volunteers used irregular warfare and guerrilla tactics to raid their former neighbors in the Mohawk Valley. They would fight in regular combat at the Battle of Oriskany, the Battle of Cobleskill, the Attack on German Flatts, the Battle of Minisink and the Battle of Newtown. Brant's Volunteers, despite their small numbers as a fighting force, were known for their brutality on the battlefield and for their actions during the Burning of the Valleys campaign, particularly for their actions during the raid and massacre at Cherry Valley, of which Brant would come to harbor disdain for his actions.

At the time of the war's end, Brant and his actions were so well known and respected that he became recognized as a senior leader of the Six Nations, and with this status, he led a large number of Six Nations families and others who allied with him to create a settlement in Ontario, where there is still a sizeable Amerindian population today. However, Brant's life in Canada postwar was not one of ease, as he found himself engaged in disputes between his own people, other Native nations, the Department of Indian Affairs, Lieutenant Governor of Upper Canada John Graves Simcoe, the government of Canada, the government of Great Britain and others. He struggled with attempting to bring peace between the Six Nations and the Western Nations, but this dream of his to build one strong Native nation faded away. Brant died in Upper Canada in 1807 at sixty-four years old.

THE QUEEN'S LOYAL RANGERS

At the time of the Seven Years' War and the American Revolution, there were several battalions throughout New York known as the Queen's Loyal Rangers or the Queen's American Rangers. On Long Island, these battalions were under the command of Robert Rogers of Seven Years' War fame in Upstate New York and then under command of John Graves Simcoe, famous for his dealings trying to put an end to the secretive Culper Spy Ring and later for his position as lieutenant governor of Upper Canada in the 1790s.

This battalion of Queen's Loyal Rangers, however, was under the command of John Peters. Peters was born in 1740 in Connecticut but would come to settle in Moorestown in New York. (Today, this is located in Vermont.) Peters was appointed a member of the Continental Congress in 1774 but chose to remain loyal to Great Britain. In 1776, he fled to Canada as many Loyalists in New York would do and, upon his arrival, was appointed to the position of colonel of the Queen's Loyal Rangers by Sir Guy Carleton, then governor of Quebec. The Queen's Loyal Rangers under Peters was present during Burgoyne's 1777 Campaign and was engaged in combat with the Americans at the Battle of Bennington.

After the war, much like other Loyalists, his property was confiscated by the new American government for his participation on the side of the British during the Revolution. Also, much like other Loyalists, he and his family would settle in Canada at the war's end. In the mid-1780s, Peters and his uncle traveled to England to submit a petition for reimbursement for his property losses as a result of remaining loyal to the Crown. He was still in England when he passed away in the late 1780s, and his uncle took his place pursuing the petition for reimbursement by the British government.

THE KING'S LOYAL AMERICANS

The King's Loyal Americans was one of the longer-lasting battalions during the American Revolution. The Loyal Americans was raised in 1776 and was commanded by Ebenezer Jessup and would later come under the command of his brother Edward. The Jessup brothers were prominent figures in Upstate New York; the pair would purchase large tracts of land around Glens Falls, about forty-five miles north of Albany. This tract of land, known as the Jessup Patent, was purchased by Sir William Johnson and the Mohawk Nation and would become the townships of Lake Luzerne, Corinth, Warrensburg, Thurman, Chestertown and Johnsburg.

Both of the brothers served in the Seven Years' War and would maintain their Loyalist ties throughout the American Revolution. It was these Loyalist ties that would get the Jessup brothers in trouble with the Patriots—like other Loyalists at the time of the Revolution, the Jessups were wanted for arrest by the Patriots and would both flee to Canada with their families in 1776. The following year, both brothers were involved in General John Burgoyne's 1777 Campaign in Upstate New York and were present at Burgoyne's surrender at Saratoga. With Burgoyne's surrender, the King's Loyal Americans made its way to Quebec, where it worked on constructing fortifications in Montreal and the lower Lake Champlain region. Ebenezer remained in Quebec with his family, but Governor Haldimand awarded Edward the title of major commandant of a new corps—Jessup's Corps of Loyal Rangers, sometimes referred to as Jessup's Rangers. Jessup's Rangers participated in Christopher Carleton's 1780 raid in Upstate New York against Fort Anne, Fort George, Queensbury, Kingsbury and Ballston Spa (then known as Ball's Town). In 1781, Edward Jessup led a number of small raids on the New York frontier, including his own raids on Queensbury, Glens Falls and Kingsbury. Besides the raids they conducted, the rangers worked on the same tasks as the King's Loyal Americans, the constructing of British fortifications, which they did until they were disbanded at the end of December 1783.

At the end of the Revolution, with the American victory, the Jessups and the Loyal Rangers would settle in Canada along the St. Lawrence River and establish townships through the purchasing of land grants. Both Edward and Ebenezer would pass away in the 1810s.

McAlpin's Corps of American Volunteers

The Burgoyne campaign of 1777 saw the rise of numerous battalions, and McAlpin's Corps of American Volunteers was just one of the many. The corps was under the command of Daniel McAlpin and was first mustered to action in August 1777, under the authorization of Sir William Howe. At the time he was mustered into action to command the Corps of American Volunteers, McAlpin was a retired British army captain and a major landowner in Stillwater, New York (near modern-day Schuylerville).

After the colonies declared independence from Britain, McAlpin was one of the Loyalists who was pursued by the Patriots for his arrest. For a time, McAlpin lay low and began secretly recruiting for the Corps of American Volunteers; however, he was arrested by the Patriots but would manage to escape and go into hiding. In the summer of 1777, when Burgoyne and the British army were marching toward Albany, McAlpin and the men he managed to raise for his Corps of American Volunteers joined with the army as they marched through Fort Edward, New York.

McAlpin's Corps of American Volunteers was one of the smaller battalions participating in the American Revolution in Upstate New York. At 184 men, the corps primarily participated in Burgoyne's 1777 Campaign by defending the British supply lines. After the Battle of Freeman's Farm, the first of the two engagements at Saratoga Battlefield, a percentage of McAlpin's corps were drafted into regular regiments to attempt to offset the heavy British casualties suffered during the engagement. After the Battle of Bemis Heights, the second engagement at Saratoga Battlefield, General Burgoyne allowed many Loyalist troops the opportunity to make their escape before his surrender in October 1777. During this escape, McAlpin's corps was entrusted with getting Burgoyne's military pay chest to Canada unmolested by the Americans. On the retreat, 50 of McAlpin's men were captured by the Americans, but the pay chest was safely and successfully delivered to Canada.

Once the Loyalist troops of Burgoyne's fighting force arrived in Canada, the Corps of American Volunteers was assembled into a battalion, and the men were trained by Sir John Johnson before command was returned to Daniel McAlpin, who was awarded the rank of major commandant. Like Jessup's Rangers, McAlpin's corps was engaged in the construction of fortifications to protect Quebec against another possible American invasion.

In late 1779, Daniel McAlpin fell ill. Despite his old age and his illness, he continued his military service until his death in the summer of 1780. Upon

Above and opposite: Merchants prepared to sell their wares to the soldiers. *Marie D.A. Williams.*

his death, he was replaced by Major John Nairne of the Eighth Regiment of Foot, who organized the corps into formal companies.

In November 1781, McAlpin's Corps of American Volunteers, the King's Loyal Americans and the Queen's Loyal Rangers were combined to form a new provincial regiment called the Loyal Rangers, under the command of Major Edward Jessup.

After participating in a series of raids in Upstate New York in 1781, the Loyal Rangers, including the former McAlpin's Corps of American Volunteers, was mustered out of service in December 1783 and established several townships in Ontario, Canada.

THE EIGHTY-FOURTH REGIMENT OF FOOT

The Eighty-Fourth Regiment of Foot, also known as the Royal Highland Emigrants, was raised to defend Ontario from the constant American attacks. The Eighty-Fourth Regiment was involved in numerous military actions in the American colonies, including raiding areas along Lake Champlain and in the Mohawk Valley. This regiment had one of the most experienced fighting forces in North America, as it was raised from Scottish soldiers who fought in the Seven Years' War and stayed in North America after the war's end. The Eighty-Fourth was organized into two battalions, with Colonel Allan Maclean commanding the first and Major General John Small commanding the second. These two battalions, however, acted independently of each other and did not see much action together.

Colonel Allan Maclean was tasked with recruiting the men for the Eighty-Fourth Regiment and was assigned to recruit for five battalions. The act of raising a British regiment in the thirteen colonies was a dangerous mission— if the recruiter was discovered, he could be executed. Maclean had made his way to New York shortly after the war had broken out and was warned that if he attempted to recruit men while in uniform, he could be killed. Because of this warning, Maclean disguised himself as a doctor. Due to the danger involved in recruiting for British regiments, the Eighty-Fourth Regiment consisted of the only two previously mentioned battalions instead of the five that were commissioned by General Thomas Gage.

Under Maclean, the first battalion of the Eighty-Fourth Regiment acted to defend Quebec from American invasions and was present during the famed Siege of Fort St. Jean, where American brigadier general Richard Montgomery launched the invasion. The first battalion made two failed attempts to relieve Fort St. Jean from the American onslaught, but the first battalion would eventually return to Quebec to help evacuate the civilians and await Guy Carleton's return from Montreal. Apart from assisting the civilians of Quebec to evacuate the city, the first battalion of the Eighty-Fourth was involved in the Battle of Quebec. During the battle, 120 men of the Eighty-Fourth and 60 Royal Navy sailors fought against American New Hampshire troops commanded by Henry Dearborn. The Eighty-Fourth was able to overwhelm the New Hampshire troops and forced them to surrender. Later in the Revolution, the first battalion of the Eighty-Fourth participated in raids in the Lake Champlain region in 1778, as well as raids in the Mohawk Valley region from 1780 through 1782.

After the American victory at the Battle of Yorktown in Virginia, which brought an end to the war, members of the Eighty-Fourth Regiment of Foot would settle in various areas of Nova Scotia, including Halifax, as well as parts of Ontario; others would leave North America entirely and immigrate to Britain in the mid-1780s.

An interesting note about the Eighty-Fourth Regiment of Foot was that, at the time of the Revolution, it was the only Highland regiment allowed to wear traditional Highland uniform, including tartan plaids and swords.

THE LOYAL FORESTERS

The Loyal Foresters was the smallest and least known of the British regiments that served in New York's colonial borders during the Revolution.

The Loyal Foresters was raised to serve with Guy Johnson and was an integrated fighting force, with whites and Amerindians alike making up its miniscule ranks. Its commanding officer, Lieutenant Colonel John Connolly, was captured by the Americans in the fall of 1775, before he was able to use his force in raids. The number of men who enlisted never exceeded twenty.

THE DESCRIPTIONS OF THE formation of these units and their actions during the war as outlined in this chapter are fairly detailed; however, these histories are complicated because the British did not keep accurate and complete records of their Loyalist regiments. The histories of these regiments are further complicated by the fact that many of these regiments had come and gone—they were usually small in number and were tasked with completing the mundane work of building and manning fortifications, cutting wood, guarding wood cutting parties, police patrolling and other duties. The smaller regiments were usually combined with larger ones, and the names of the regiments and their commanding officers often changed, or the regiments were known by multiple names.

For the British, the American Revolution was a civil war and was seen as such even beyond the writing of the Declaration of Independence, and due to this view on the war, the North American Loyalists and the British-born troops were treated differently by the Crown. The North American Loyalists were better than their British-born counterparts at the process of recruiting new troops. The better the Loyalists were at convincing others to join the war effort, the quicker they were to form regiments and move up in the ranks to earn their captaincies and colonelcies and other officer rankings. Despite the unequal treatment, regular British army officers were envious of their North American counterparts. Whereas their own promotions and commissions were tied into their family wealth and history, the North American Loyalists could acquire these same commissions and promotions through their actions during the Revolution; however, the North American Loyalists were not awarded battle honors as the individual soldiers and regiments that fought in the Revolution because of the Crown's view of the Revolution as a civil war. But battle honors

British soldiers overlooking the battlefield. *Marie D.A. Williams.*

were awarded to those who fought against America's French, Spanish and Dutch allies in the West Indies and in other theaters of the war.

The Loyalist regiments were sometimes desegregated; several regiments recruited free blacks and escaped slaves who, after Lord Dunmore's Proclamation, were offered their freedom in exchange for joining the British. Officers of these integrated regiments were white, but the regiments themselves had both white and nonwhite troops in the ranks. While these integrated regiments did see some military action, they were usually involved in the mundane tasks of cleaning, cooking, digging fortifications and other such tasks.

ALTHOUGH THERE IS MORE information about some regiments than there is regarding others, as a whole these regiments all played a role, sometimes minor and other times major, in the destructive raids on New York's wilderness and frontier settlements in the Champlain, Hudson and Mohawk Valley regions. The men in the regiments served the purpose of inducing fear and uncertainty in the people who resided in the affected areas, and

Camp followers feeding a young soldier. *Marie D.A. Williams.*

they accomplished this through the burning of crops and farmhouses and the dismantling and destruction of various types of mills to disrupt the flow of food, weapons, munitions and more to the American forces. These regiments, through their raids, would lower the morale of the Patriots in the areas they attacked and force them to flee from their homes. However, the Patriots would not take these raids lightly and would eventually carry out their own raids against Loyalist and Amerindian settlements in New York to disrupt the flow of the supplies for the British armies.

The different Loyalist and British forces that made their wartime home in New York, and who may have made New York their home prior to the outbreak of the war, played a major role in the various raids in the state's colonial borders. The need to delineate the groups from one another is tantamount to the of the remainder of this monograph as the groups sometimes combined with one another and sometimes seemingly acted of their own accord, as will be seen in later passages.

3

THE KING'S NATIVES

The various Loyalist forces described in detail in the previous chapter were not the only forces employed by the British in their raiding campaigns against the New York frontier. The king's men also consisted of warriors from the Six Nations of the Iroquois.

The Haudenosaunee, as the Iroquois called themselves, were a powerful Native American confederacy. Once known as the Five Nations, in 1722 the Iroquois Confederacy accepted the Tuscarora into their confederacy and the confederacy became the Six Nations. The six nations of the Iroquois were the Mohawk, Onondaga, Oneida, Cayuga, Seneca and Tuscarora.

The Iroquois began building a lasting relationship with the British in the 1750s as both Britain and France worked to gain the Six Nations as allies in the Seven Years' War. While the French had some initial success with the Senecas, the Six Nations ultimately sided with the British. If a single man could be attributed to the alliance, that man would be Sir William Johnson. Johnson would become the superintendent of Indian Affairs and would spend his life working to maintain the British-Iroquois relationship. This relationship led to the British victory at the conclusion of the Seven Years' War.

The peace that came with the conclusion of the Seven Years' War was short-lived as the colonists began pushing further and further into Native lands; Six Nations and British colonial leaders met at Fort Stanwix in 1768 to discuss a firm boundary line between the British American colonies and the Native landholdings. The treaty would do little to quell the colonists from pushing into the Native territories, believing that they fought for the land in the Seven Years' War and that their victory meant they had a right

Mohawk warriors on their way to the British military drills. *Marie D.A. Williams.*

to that land. With the staggering costs of the war and the Crown raising taxes and implementing new laws for the colonists to follow, along with the inability to reside on the land they had fought for during the previous armed conflict, a growing rift was formed between the American colonists and the British Crown, and the Natives, particularly the Six Nations, would be drawn into another war.

The Six Nations were not initially drawn into the conflict that would become the American War of Independence. In fact, the Six Nations did not understand why the colonists were fighting among themselves and had little interest in being drawn into what they saw as a civil war. In the early days of the American Revolution, however, leaders of the Oneida Nation declared their neutrality in the war by sending a message to the New York governor stating that regardless of whether the Crown or the Colonies sought their aid, they would refuse to aid both sides. However, the course of neutrality chosen by the Six Nations could not be maintained for long, and the Six Nations, and individuals therein, would be forced to choose sides. The majority of the Six Nations, with the exception of the Oneida and the Tuscarora, chose to ally themselves with the British to keep in line with the old alliance system, and the Nations believed that their landholdings would be better protected if they sided with the British and the British won.

The Iroquois would play monumental roles in the American Revolution, particularly in New York. The Mohawk, specifically, would be of paramount importance in the British campaign in New York. Two notable Mohawks who played important roles at this time were siblings Joseph and Molly Brant. Joseph Brant would lead numerous raids on New York's frontier settlements throughout the war.

MOHAWK

During the American Revolution, most of the Mohawks lived along the Mohawk River in New York, living in such places as Canajoharie, Schoharie and Fort Hunter. The Mohawk were among four of the six Iroquois nations to side with the British during the war. They had a long-standing trading relationship with the British and had hoped that by siding with the British, there would be an end to the colonists encroaching on their land in the Mohawk River Valley. Joseph Brant acted as a war chief and would lead various successful raids against the localities that supported the Patriots.

Although the Mohawks were known as supporters of the British, a few prominent Mohawk leaders, such as the sachem Tyorhansera, remained neutral throughout the war. Other prominent Mohawk leaders, such as Joseph Louis Cook, a veteran of the Seven Years' War, would offer their services to the Americans.

Oneida

The Oneida played a major role in the American Revolution, siding with the Patriots against the British. Although the Oneida Nation initially declared their neutrality in what they deemed a civil war, warriors later fought in several key battles in the Revolution, including the Battles of Oriskany and Saratoga. They became known as America's first allies.

The Oneida were able to provide the most physical support during the war, especially from 1777 to 1778. They were present at the Battle of Oriskany during the Saratoga Campaign prior to the start of the frontier raids. The Oneida even provided warriors to General Horatio Gates and to General George Washington, with some warriors even staying at Valley Forge in the winter of 1778.

The primary role of the Oneida to the Americans during the war was as scouts, guides and couriers—largely support roles—but were nonetheless important, as these roles allowed the Americans to gain intelligence on the British military movements and to receive aid from nearby regiments. Along with these roles, the Oneida were engaged in scouting expeditions to Oswego and were engaged in raids against the Iroquois nations who sided with the British.

Maybe surprisingly, the Oneida were reluctant participants in the Sullivan-Clinton Expedition of 1779 against the Iroquois, who had chosen to side with the British. The Oneida also provided scouts to counter the British raids in the Hudson and Mohawk Valleys.

Toward the end of the Revolution, the Oneida had lost a great deal due to the decision to side with the Americans. One of their villages had been destroyed, and the nation had to move to the areas of Oriskany and Schenectady for safety. By 1780, some of the surviving Oneida were forced to change their alliance to side with the British to protect themselves and their families. By the end of the fighting in 1783, the Oneida Nation had lost homes, any wealth they possessed and their overall way of life. They had few resources to fall back on to subsist, and it was not until the 1790s that the Oneida received any recompense for their service to the Americans in the war. Between the Oneida and the Tuscarora, the U.S. government paid out around $5,000 total to cover the destruction of the homes and crops of their Native American allies.

ONONDAGA

In the American Revolution, the Onondaga were neutral at first. However, just as other Natives had done, individual Onondaga warriors participated in raids against the Americans and their settlements in the New York frontier. The Onondaga as a whole were pulled out of their pact of neutrality after the Americans attacked their main villages in April 1779 and sided with the British for the remainder of the war.

At the conclusion of the Revolution, many Onondaga followed Joseph Brant and his Mohawks to reside in Upper Canada, where the Crown gave them land for their loyalty in the war.

CAYUGA

The Cayuga were caught in the middle of the Revolution in New York, with some fighting for the British, some for the Americans and others choosing to remain neutral. However, the Cayuga, above all, were loyal to their families and to their land, and as both the Americans and the British encroached on their land, the Cayuga defended themselves.

In 1779, General George Washington commissioned Generals John Sullivan and James Clinton to destroy Iroquois villages in western New York, and the Cayuga were heavily affected, as their homes and crops were destroyed. After the war, many individual Cayuga relocated to Ohio and/or Canada, but those who remained negotiated the Treaty of Canandaigua with the United States in the 1790s. This provided for the sovereignty of the Six Nations and established the reach of the federal government over New York State.

SENECA

When the American Revolution broke out, the Seneca attempted to remain neutral, just as the other Iroquois nations intended, but both sides attempted to bring the Seneca into the action. At the Battle of Oriskany, when the Americans defeated the British at Fort Stanwix, they killed many Seneca warriors and onlookers. This event, along with the anti–Native American rhetoric of the Americans, pushed the Seneca to side with the British.

The Seneca and the other Iroquois nations who sided with the British were involved in numerous notable battles and raids in the New York frontier. Although the Seneca, and the Iroquois as a whole, were active participants in the Revolution, prominent leaders such as Cornplanter and Blacksnake were disgusted by the brutality of the war and the mental toll of killing so many people and spoke out against their own actions.

The Seneca suffered at the hands of the Americans during the notorious Sullivan Expedition. After the expedition, the Seneca and other warriors renewed their raids on the American settlements in New York, as well as on Oneida and Tuscarora settlements, even continuing these raids after the British surrendered at Yorktown. The warriors stopped fighting in 1782, pending the peace negotiations between the British and the Americans.

At the conclusion of the war, the Seneca and other Iroquois nations were required to cede all of their lands in New York, just as the British were required to cede territories in the thirteen colonies to the new United States.

TUSCARORA

The entrance of the Tuscarora into the American Revolution was a unique set of circumstances. The Tuscarora, unlike the other five Iroquois Nations, were not originally from New York. Prior to 1713, the Tuscarora inhabited the Carolinas but fled for New York to join the Iroquois Confederacy after an event that would be called the Tuscarora War.

Finding information about the actions the Tuscarora nation took during the American Revolution is not an easy feat; however, there is an abundance of information about the monetary and proprietary claims made by Tuscarora individuals in the wake of the Revolution. According to a document discovered by historian Lyman Draper, who interviewed individuals about the American Revolution in the 1800s, there were only eight Tuscarora individuals/families who claimed losses at the conclusion of the war, with several other claimants being Oneida Natives. The document not only lists the claimed losses but also lists individual accounts describing how these individuals lived during the war. Most of the claimants lost horses and/or other livestock and at least one house. Others, however, claimed more items, highlighting that the area in which they lived had been burned during a raid, which was common practice, as will be evidenced later in this narrative. Oneida and Tuscarora individuals also attempted to make fraudulent claims that belongings were destroyed or taken, when it would later be proven that those individuals were not in the location where they supposedly lost their belongings.

The Tuscarora had sided with the Americans during the Revolution. Of those who played a role in the Continental army, some served as warriors while others served as intelligence gatherers, able to collect information on the British movements with their own warriors. One prominent Tuscarora Native was Nicholas Cusick. Cusick served in the American Revolution for a total of five years, gathering intelligence on enemy Indian groups and their movements for the Americans. He, along with a man named Johannas Oosterhout Jr., submitted a detailed and lengthy report to the New York Council of Safety in August 1777.

THE AMERICAN REVOLUTION WOULD destroy the once great power of the Six Nations. During the war, as a response to four of the six nations siding with the British and for the raids they participated in, commander-in-chief of the Continental army George Washington sent an expeditionary force under Generals John Sullivan and James Clinton into central and western New York with the sole purpose of destroying enemy Iroquois property at Unadilla and Onaquaga. After the Revolution, many of the remaining Iroquois would settle in Canada, just as many remaining Loyalists would do as well.

The participation of the Iroquois, especially when it came to the raids in New York's frontier, was paramount to the success or failure of the raids and of the war in its entirety. The need to delineate between the Six Nations and their reasons for choosing sides was tantamount to understanding the remainder of this narrative. Through the later chapters of this work, readers will encounter the various nations and their wartime actions, as well as important figures who played varied roles during the wilderness raids of 1778 through 1783.

The actions taken by the Iroquois during the American Revolution would help shape the course of the war in New York, especially when it came to the wilderness raids from 1778 until the war's end. The four nations that sided with the British were able to successfully assist in perpetrating the raids, but their actions were not without consequences, as the Oneida, who conducted their own raids against their fellow Iroquois, would experience.

4

SIR GUY CARLETON
IN UPSTATE NEW YORK

After the British defeat at the conclusion of the Saratoga Campaign, the British under John Burgoyne and others would retreat north to what would become modern-day Canada and to Boston, Massachusetts, where the army would winter. As the British pulled out of New York in various directions, a plan was underway by the British in Quebec and other would-be provinces to conduct raids in the frontier wilderness areas of Upstate New York, attacking forts and villages that could provide food, clothing, shelter, weapons and ammunition for the Continental army. These raids, largely unknown to the New York public today, brought devastation and uncertainty to the areas in which they occurred. One such commanding officer during these events was General Sir Guy Carleton, who would carry out his own military excursions in the Lake Champlain region of Upstate New York beginning in the year 1775, before plans for raiding New York had been made by the British; however, Sir Guy Carleton's excursions, along with the British defeat at Saratoga, would prove to be a jumping-off point for the British raids to come.

SIR GUY CARLETON WAS born in Strabane, Ireland, in September 1724 and was the son of Christopher and Catherine Carleton. On May 21, 1742, Carleton was accepted as an ensign in the Twenty-Fifth Regiment of Foot. He rose through the ranks and was promoted to the rank of lieutenant in 1745 and would work to further his military career by joining the First Foot Guards in July 1751. During his time in the First Foot Regiment, Guy Carleton befriended Major James Wolfe, and in 1752, Wolfe would recommend Carleton to the Duke of Richmond to be a military tutor. The relationship he built with the Duke of Richmond would allow Carleton to build relationships with other influential people of the time; for example, during the Seven Years' War, Carleton was appointed to the position of aide-de-camp to the Duke of Cumberland and had obtained the rank of lieutenant colonel. After having this role for a year, Carleton was made a lieutenant colonel in the Duke of Richmond's new Seventy-Second Foot regiment.

Carleton continued to play a role in the Seven Years' War and came under the command of James Wolfe in 1758, with Wolfe now in the rank of brigadier general. In September 1759, Carleton took part in the Battle of Quebec but was injured during the fighting and returned to Britain to recover for a time. In 1962, Carleton was promoted to the rank of colonel and was transferred to the Ninety-Sixth Foot after the Seven Years' War came to an end.

With the war's end, Carleton found himself in a new role as lieutenant governor and administrator of Quebec in April 1766. Carleton clashed with Governor James Murray over matters of government reform, and once Murray resigned, he was appointed the captain general and governor in chief of Quebec in April 1768. Over the course of his term, Carleton worked to implement reforms and improve the economy of the province. Carleton opposed the British legislature's determination to form a colonial assembly in Canada and sailed to Britain in August 1770 to press his case in person, which led to the crafting of the Quebec Act of 1774. The Quebec Act of 1774 extended the boundaries of the province and guaranteed religious freedom to Catholic Canadians.

In September 1774, Carleton returned to the province of Quebec. At the time, tensions between the American colonies and Great Britain were running high, as many of the American colonists were against the taxes the Crown was imposing to pay for the Seven Years' War. Carleton, who at this time was given the rank of major general, was ordered by Major General Thomas Gage to dispatch two Canadian regiments to Boston, where the bulk of the colonial protests were occurring at the time. As a result of having to dispatch the two regiments, Carleton offset this loss in troops by working to raise additional troops in Quebec. Some new

Sir Guy Carleton. *Library of Congress.*

troops were assembled, but Carleton was underwhelmed by the numbers, as Canadians were unwilling to rally for the Crown. In May 1775, the American Revolution was underway, and Americans were moving close to Canada, particularly to the province of Quebec, with Colonels Benedict Arnold and Ethan Allen moving to capture Fort Ticonderoga between Lake George and Lake Champlain. Carleton realized that the Americans were moving to invade Canada in the summer of 1775 and moved the bulk of his forces to Montreal and Fort St. Jean to attempt to block the American advance north from Lake Champlain to Quebec.

The Americans under Brigadier General Richard Montgomery would lay siege to Fort St. Jean in September 1775. Carleton attempted to relieve the fort, but his efforts failed, and the fort fell to Montgomery on November

3, 1775. Carleton abandoned Montreal with the falling of Fort St. Jean and withdrew his forces to Quebec but found that an American force under Colonel Benedict Arnold was already in the area and would be joined in December by the forces under Brigadier General Montgomery.

Carleton worked to improve Quebec's defenses in anticipation of an American assault; the assault would occur on December 30 and 31, 1775, as the Battle of Quebec. Carleton and his men were successful in this battle, Brigadier General Montgomery was killed and the Americans failed in taking the city. Reinforcements arrived in May 1776, and Arnold's troops retreated toward Montreal and moved south along the Richelieu River toward Lake Champlain, with Carleton's troops at his heels. This would ensue in the Battle of Valcour Island.

In October 1776, the British under the command of General John Burgoyne were planning to invade America through Canada via Lake Champlain, where they would then be able to take the Hudson River to Albany. Under General William Howe, as well as his brother Admiral Richard Howe, the British took New York City, and the southern British army under General Howe made its way north up the Hudson River to Albany; together, the combined forces of Burgoyne and Howe would capture New York. Realizing that Lake Champlain and Lake George would be the British army's gateway to the north, the Americans made a commitment to stop the British advance on the lakes. As the British army began its advance, General John Sullivan and Benedict Arnold wrote to George Washington, urging that Lake Champlain should be secured by an American naval fleet. At Skenesborough (later renamed Whitehall), Sullivan, Arnold and Major General Philip Schuyler constructed the first American naval force using the iron forge and sawmills in the town. On October 11, 1776, as part of the American naval force lay in wait in Valcour Bay, they were alerted to the oncoming British fleet, which unbeknownst to the Americans, was superior to their own, having twice as many cannons, more ships and more men who were trained sailors. As the British and the Americans engaged in a naval battle in Valcour Bay, the British fired on the Americans from Valcour Island itself, as well as the shore of Lake Champlain. The American fleet was so crippled from the battle that Arnold and his generals made the decision to escape to Fort Crown Point under the cover of darkness.

However, the Americans and the British would engage each other again. The results would be devastating for the Americans and would bring destruction to nearby homes—one home, belonging to a Patriot family headed by a man named Peter Ferris, was reportedly hit by several cannonballs and grapeshot. As a consequence of assisting the Americans escape into the woods after their fleet was run aground, the British burned the Ferris home and farm and killed all of the cattle therein. The social implications of the Americans' failed attempt at the Battle of Valcour Island were the destruction of property by citizens who helped and supported the Patriot forces. Sir Guy Carleton and his nephew Sir Christopher Carleton, who were both involved in the Battle of Valcour Island, would carry out raids in Upstate New York, destroying towns and villages where Patriots resided or where the Patriot forces could potentially obtain help from the local population.

Although the Americans lost the Battle of Valcour Island and the British under the Carletons would carry out raids against American towns, what the battle did accomplish was that it would be too late in the year for the British to attempt to fight the Americans in Upstate New York again. In the summer of 1777, however, prior to the events of the Saratoga Campaign, the Americans and the British would engage each other one more time at Fort Ticonderoga.

In June, the British under Burgoyne began to make their way from Canada to Albany, continuing the attack plan that Britain initially invented to take New York and divide the colonies. In early July, Burgoyne was ready to retake Fort Ticonderoga from the Americans, who not only fortified the fort but also the nearby Mount Hope. Mount Defiance, which overlooked the fort, was left undefended, and the British used it to their benefit by secretly sending engineers up the mountain to clear an area for artillery on the siege of the fort. The British position on Mount Defiance, however, was discovered, and the Americans made the decision to retreat from the fort and give up their strategic location rather than engage with the British. As the Americans made their retreat, leading two hundred boats south through Skenesborough, as well as heading through Mount Independence, the British were able to retake Fort Ticonderoga without firing a single shot, like their American counterparts of 1775, but they would attack the Americans as they made their retreat.

As a response to the end of the siege at Fort Ticonderoga, General Philip Schuyler wrote letters to General Washington to tell him of the loss and how valiantly the men fought. However, the letters also indicated that the men lost everything they possessed at the siege and inquired of Washington to send "Tents for 4,000 Men, 500 Camp Kettles: a Quantity of fixed musket Ammunition, Cartridge-paper 12 pieces heavy Cannon with travelling Carriages 16 Field pieces and a considerable Quantity of

Ammunition for them; a competent Number of Artillery Men, in Addition to Major Steven's Corps, so as to be sufficient to manage the Artillery; All the Implements necessary to the Artillery; Horses, Harness and Drivers; about 600 Intrenching Tools sorted, excluding pick axes of which we have a considerable Number."

It was true that the Americans lost everything in the siege, but it was also true that military gear was not easy to come by. The Continental Congress had failed to provide the Continental army with the necessities it needed at the time of the war, such as gear, money and even the number of able-bodied men willing to fight and die for the idea of America. The Americans would be underpaid, undermanned and undersupplied for the duration of the war—only achieving some relief after the Battle of Saratoga, with the help of the French, Spanish and Dutch.

Although it was another loss for the Americans in Upstate New York, the events of the siege of Fort Ticonderoga continued to slow the British march toward Albany, and the events of the Saratoga Campaign would play out. The remainder of this chapter discusses the events of the Saratoga Campaign and the social effects of the series of battles on the population of the surrounding areas.

In 1777, command of the campaign south into New York was granted to Major General John Burgoyne. In his anger, Carleton resigned his position in the British military but was forced to remain in his position for another year until his replacement arrived. In that time, Burgoyne was defeated at the Battle of Saratoga and was forced to surrender, as described in the first chapter. In mid-1778, Carleton returned to Britain and was appointed to the Commission of Public Accounts in 1780. Because the war was going poorly for the British with General Sir Henry Clinton as the commander-in-chief of the British forces in North America, Sir Guy Carleton was granted the position and would replace General Clinton in 1782. Carleton arrived in New York in August 1783, as Britain was making moves toward peace. Carleton oversaw the evacuation of British forces, Loyalists and freed slaves who had joined the British from New York City.

In 1786, Carleton was granted governorship of Quebec, Nova Scotia and New Brunswick in Canada. He would remain in these posts until 1796, when he retired to his estate in Hampshire, England. He passed away in November 1808.

THE ACTIONS OF SIR Guy Carleton played a huge role in the American Revolution and the British actions in Upstate New York, and his actions, and nonactions on the part of the Crown, bring up several questions as to what may have happened had Carleton been granted the position held by General John Burgoyne or been granted the position of commander-in-chief of the British forces in North America sooner. Despite these lingering questions about events and actions past, Carleton would pass on the role of leading forces to his nephew Christopher Carleton, who would lead forces in raids in the wilderness frontier areas of New York congruently with the Jessup brothers, Edward and Ebenezer, as well as with John Johnson and Joseph Brant.

THE CHRISTOPHER CARLETON RAIDS

In 1749, Christopher Carleton was born in Newcastle upon Tyne, England, into a military family. His parents died at sea when Christopher was four years old, and his uncles, Sir Guy Carleton and Sir Thomas Carleton, saw that he was educated and brought up well for the era. Christopher Carleton joined the British army as an ensign in the Thirty-First Regiment of Foot at the age of twelve. His entrance into the military saw him off to North America, where he met Sir William Johnson of Battle of Lake George and Johnson Hall fame, and who provided Christopher with the opportunity to live among the Mohawk Indians in New York. The younger Carleton learned their language and participated in their customs. As a member of the British military in New York, the knowledge he gained while living among the Mohawks served him well, and he would have the opportunity to have Mohawk warriors among his future troops.

Over the course of his life, the younger Carleton would recount the time he had spent living among the Mohawks, and even other officers would recount that Carleton was happiest among them, living their way of life. In the mid-1770s, Carleton lived among the Natives at Kahnawake and Kanehsatake. He took an Indian wife but would later marry his uncle Guy's sister-in-law. He became involved in village politics, developed lasting friendships with the Natives and, overall, gained their trust, which would allow connections between the Natives and the British in Canada to foster and grow and would lead to Carleton commanding a blended force of Native warriors and British troops.

In May 1776, Captain Christopher Carleton was called to Quebec City as part of a relief force for his uncle Sir Guy Carleton during the Battle of Quebec, where the Americans were besieging the city. As the Americans retreated after the siege, Captain Carleton assisted his uncle in following them and led a force of Native Americans against the Americans at the Battle of Valcour Island. After the Battle of Valcour Island, Captain Carleton purchased a major's commission and served under his uncle Sir Thomas Carleton in the Twenty-Ninth Regiment of Foot.

Beginning in 1778, Major Christopher Carleton led a series of raids in Upstate New York, starting in the Lake Champlain area, with orders to destroy all supplies, animals, provisions and more that the Americans had assembled on the shores of the lake. Other orders included taking citizens who had sworn allegiance to the Continental Congress and destroying all of the boats Carleton's men could discover, as well as sawmills and gristmills that could be beneficial to the American cause. The purpose for the first raids in 1778 was that the British were concerned that the Americans would be able to use their supplies against the British forces, particularly that the Americans would be able to access any supplies stored in the Crown Point and Ticonderoga areas.

Carleton's expedition forces arrived at Valcour Island on October 2, 1778, and they were joined by the Fort Hunter Mohawk party and a group known as Claus' Rangers. The next day, the groups set sail down the Richelieu River. Some groups were sent to Johnstown and Ball's Town (now Ballston Spa) to gather intelligence, and Carleton sent scouts; his parties ran into two Native Americans, who, when asked if they were on their way to join Carleton, replied that they were. The scouts returned to Carleton and told him of their encounter, describing the Native Americans they saw as being physically fatigued. Carleton and others were concerned about the identities of the men, with the primary belief being that they may have been rebel Oneida Indians. A party of scouts from nearby Fort Hunter were sent to search for the two Native Americans who were seen by the first scouting party, but the search was unsuccessful. That same afternoon, Lieutenant William Johnson of the Forty-Seventh Regiment and seconded to the Quebec Indian Department arrived in Split Rock, where Carleton and forces were located, with 108 Canadian Indians from the towns of Kahnawake and Kanehsatake. Johnson also brought word that Lieutenant Richard Houghton, who was also seconded to the Quebec Indian Department, had taken the majority of the Canadian Indians from St. John's to Connecticut to attempt to distract the American forces.

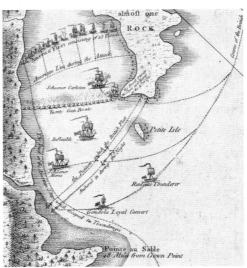

Above: Cannons over the northern end of Lake George in Upstate New York. *Marie D.A. Williams.*

Right: The movements of the Battle of Valcour Island, 1776. *America's Historic Lakes.*

On October 6, Carleton's forces left Split Rock and sailed to south of Crown Point, where they would keep up regular scouting parties as they prepared to make a stealthy move toward Ticonderoga, where the Americans were holding supplies. This first raid was very successful for Carleton; the British were able to capture thirty-nine prisoners and destroy enough food stocks to last an army of twelve thousand men four months. The British also destroyed animals, homes, barns and the sawmills and gristmills in the Saratoga and Crown Point areas. This first raid, carried out with a combined force of British troops and Native American allies, would make New Yorkers fearful of Indian attacks and raids, which they had experience with in the past but not to the extent they were experiencing with the raids during the American Revolution.

CARLETON'S RAID WOULD CONTINUE through 1779 and 1780, and other British military leaders would conduct raids in conjunction with Carleton, such as the Burning of the Valleys. In October 1780, the forces of Major Christopher Carleton attacked several hamlets, towns and forts in Upstate New York, beginning with Fort Anne (now Fort Ann) on October 10, 1780, and proceding south to attack the areas of Kingsbury, Queensbury, Glens Falls, Fort Edward, Fort Miller and Fort George on Lake George, and a branch of his men under Captain John Munro burned Schoharie and part of Ball's Town. Over the course of this particular expedition, a recorded 148 prisoners were taken by Carleton and Munro.

Carleton was not a major player when it came to the British capture and burning of Fort Anne, Ball's Town, Kingsbury, Queensbury, Glens Falls or the others, but he did play a major role as a commanding officer during these events. Carleton advanced south along Lake Champlain with 518 British regulars, 315 Provincials from various Loyalist regiments and an unknown number of Native warriors. Serving under Carleton were Major Edward Jessup, Captain William Fraser and Captain John Munro, who were all familiar with the area they were about to enter in search of materials to destroy so the rebel Americans could not use them. For example, Edward Jessup and his brother, Ebenezer, received a large land grant from Sir William Johnson, the father of their fellow commanding officer Sir John Johnson, and the Mohawk Indians along the upper Hudson River. (Their land would become the towns of Lake Luzerne, Hadley, Corinth, Thurman, Warrensburg, Chestertown and Johnsburg.) Fraser's family purchased a lot in Ball's Town in 1772 after they emmigrated from Ireland, and Munro owned eleven thousand acres of land along the Vermont border. Besides the commanding officers of these combined forces owning land in the Upper Hudson River and Mohawk River Valleys, where they were raiding, they all knew the people who inhabited the invasion route as well as their Tory/Loyalist friends and their rebel American enemies. They could expect protection and provisions from the Loyalists in the area as they moved through the frontier land of the Hudson River Valley and the Mohawk Valley. From their American counterparts, they could expect the local militias, particularly the Albany and Tryon County militias, to harass them as they moved through the river valleys.

Carleton's main body of combined troops moved south along Lake Champlain past Fort Ticonderoga, which had not been manned by either side of the conflict since Burgoyne had surrendered at Saratoga in October 1777, moved into South Bay and arrived at Skenesborough (Whitehall) on October 8, 1780. The next day, the army proceeded south past an abandoned blockhouse and soon arrived at Fort Anne, which was defended by Captain Adiel Sherwood and his force of only seventy-four militiamen to Carleton's force of over eight hundred troops. Fort Anne and its group of defenders were small, which was typical of the forts constructed to protect New York's frontier lands from invasion. The British noticed that the fort was decrepit and severely undermanned, and Captain Sherwood and his militiamen surrendered and were taken captive by Carleton's troops.

Carleton was not finished with his series of raids. On the morning of October 11, 1780, his troops advanced toward Fort George, which was on the southern end of Lake George. The commanding officer at Fort George, Captain John Chipman, was unaware of how sizeable a force was advancing toward the fort; to gain the necessary knowledge and to assess the situation of the British advance, he sent out a scouting party of forty-eight men under Captain Thomas Sill. Sill's men, however, were quickly surrounded by Native American warriors, which resulted in a combative encounter at Bloody Pond, known for its role in the Seven Years' War, where a force of Native Americans, British and Canadian troops clashed, and the bodies of the dead were rolled into the shallow pond, staining the water a deep red. At this encounter between the British and the small contingent forces of the Americans, twenty-seven troops were killed, including Captain Sill, while eight were captured and thirteen fled into the forest.

Captain Chipman along with forty-five of his men, all from Colonel Seth Warner's Continental Regiment, were forced to surrender Fort George to the British. The prisoners were marched out of the fort, and Carleton's Native warriors were permitted to search the fort for valuables, food, weapons and ammunition. The following day, Carleton's fighting force, as well as the more than one hundred prisoners they had captured, set out northward along Lake George to return to Crown Point. They arrived at their destination by October 16 and would wait to hear from Captain Munro, who had separated from the primary group prior to the attacks in October and had not been heard from since October 6.

Also, between the dates of October 10 and October 11, Carleton's men set fire to Kingsbury and then turned to Queensbury and set fire to it as well. Carleton detached a party of the King's Rangers under the command of Lieutenant David Jones, who had lived in the garrison town around Fort Edward, as well as a second party under the command of an unknown officer who led a group of twelve King's Rangers. The goal of these two parties, as commanded by Carleton, was to destroy the garrison town of Fort Edward. The inhabitants of the garrison town had been warned of the burning of Kingsbury and Queensbury and fled the area.

When the detachment under Lieutenant Jones returned to Carleton, they brought a supply of provisions and several prisoners from their raid. Jones's detachment traveled fourteen miles south of Fort Edward and destroyed everything in their path without opposition, including the village of Fort Edward and the house of Colonel John McCrea at Fort Miller. Although on opposite sides of the war, Jones and McCrea had a connection; Jones's fiancée was Jane McCrea, who was killed near Fort Edward in July 1777, and Colonel McCrea was her older brother. The detachment of King's

Rangers under Jones was ordered to march south and destroy all they found on the east bank as far as Fort Miller and then cross the Hudson River to the west bank and burn mills and grain stores east of Saratoga.

CAPTAIN JOHN MUNRO'S RAID

Captain John Munro left Carleton's forces on October 6 from Crown Point and traveled Bullwagga Bay to begin his own march with his group of expeditionary forces. The troops under Munro were over-encumbered by their ammunition and provisions; the average soldier under Munro was carrying around seventy-five pounds of food, clothing, ammunition and his musket. Because it was necessary to move quietly through the wooded frontier areas, Munro allowed the troops to shed some of the weight, but the troops would come to regret the decision to lighten their loads, as there would be a drastic reduction in the food they were carrying. On October 7, Munro led his force of 195 men on a trail toward Saratoga, traveling along the Schroon River and then along the base of Crane Mountain and along the Hudson River, where they arrived just south of Warrensburg. From there, they reached the confluence of the Hudson and Sacandaga Rivers on October 11.

On October 11, four men who were with the Royal Yorkers under Carlton met with Munro's troops at a designated area on the Sacandaga River to inform Munro that Carleton had taken Forts Anne and George and then returned to Ticonderoga on Lake Champlain with his own troops. This knowledge of Carleton's part of the raid coming to an end was beneficial for Munro; however, runners who had been sent to inform him of the whereabouts of Sir John Johnson and his troops had not returned, so Munro was left out of the loop on that front. Also, Captain William Fraser and a Mohawk warrior had been sent out as scouts to Ball's Town to collect intelligence of the area but had failed to meet at the designated rendezvous point with Munro. Ball's Town was close to Saratoga, which was Munro's primary target at the time of his expedition, and he had heard rumors that a large number of Loyalists—wives and children of some of his troops—were being held in custody in the barracks in the town. Because of this, Munro decided to abandon his plan of heading for Saratoga and instead urged his men on to Ball's Town. Not only that, but many of the provisions that his men were carrying were dwindling, and he believed that Ball's Town would be a good secondary target for his men to raid, as they could restock their supplies. The town of Schenectady was to be a secondary area to raid, apart from Ball's Town, but Munro had decided to abandon that objective, as he judged that it would be too heavily defended by the Albany and Tryon County militias.

The plan to raid Ball's Town and the surrounding areas was settled, and it was believed that this raid could be twofold for the British: they had the opportunity to destroy the mills and foodstuffs in the community and Munro's party would have the opportunity to exact revenge on the Twelfth Regiment of the Albany County militia, which had made Ball's Town its home base, under the command of Lieutenant Colonel James Gordon and Captain Tyrannus Collins.

Lieutenant Colonel Gordon and Captain Collins were known to the British since the very beginning of the Revolution. They and the militiamen they led had been diligent in tracking down Loyalists and making life in the New York frontier miserable for them. In May 1777, they forced Major Daniel McAlpin, a local Loyalist officer, among others, to flee to Canada, confiscated property owned by Loyalists and put the wives and children of British soldiers in confinement in Albany. That same spring, Collins captured Captain William Fraser and his brother, along with forty Loyalists, who were on their way to join the British in Canada. Captain Fraser and his brother had been imprisoned in Albany but were able to escape from the prison and had successfully joined Burgoyne's forces. Lieutenant Colonel Gordon was not just a commanding officer of the Twelfth Regiment of the Albany County Militia but was also a member of the New York Assembly, where he advocated for harsh treatment of captured Loyalists in the state and was a supporter of the 1779 Confiscation Act, which called for the banishment of those who sided with the British and sentenced them to death without clemency if they returned to New York. Munro used the actions carried out by Gordon and Collins as justification for his move against Ball's Town.

Munro and his men approached Ball's Town from the (current) Galway-Milton town line, and as they moved, his troops captured two men who were believed to be acting as scouts but were quick to inform the British that they were not, claiming that they were just two friends out hunting. However, two of the Mohawk warriors traveling with Munro recognized the men in an instance that would prove fatal. The men the Mohawks recognized were John Shew and Isaac Palmatier. Shew had been captured by these same Mohawk warriors in 1778 but had managed to escape, an action that would not happen a second time. Shew was tied to a tree and bludgeoned with a tomahawk to the head; Palmatier was taken prisoner by the British.

Munro's men were met by a Loyalist sympathizer named James McDonald, who guided them through a path, later named Devil's Lane, until they came on James Gordon's property. From there, Munro divided his forces—Fraser and his Provincials would move across the Mourning Kill to the home of Captain Collins, while he and 130 of his men, flanked by 30 Mohawk warriors, would move on Gordon's home. As the men were divided to move on these two homes, it was evident that this raid was not going to be random destruction like previous raids under the British had been.

Around midnight, Munro and his men moved against Gordon. Gordon was asleep in his home with his wife, Mary, when the pair was woken by the sound of bayonets being thrust through the bedroom window. Escaping into the hallway of their home, they were confronted by a Mohawk warrior with a tomahawk raised, ready to kill, but with the intervention of Captain Munro, Colonel James Gordon was saved from death. Gordon was a man of relative means, and his household consisted of two farmhands and four slaves—one of the slaves, Jacob, served in the British army under Burgoyne but had been captured by the Americans and was taken prisoner. Gordon, his farmhands and all but one of his slaves (a woman named Liz who had managed to escape) were taken by the British.

At the time of the attack on Lieutenant Colonel Gordon's household, Fraser and his rangers were preparing to move on the home of Captain Tyrannus Collins. Captain Collins was home with his fourteen-year-old son and his female slave. Collins barred the door of his log home long enough for his son to escape through a hole in the opening of a wall on the second floor, which was intended for a future window. A tomahawk was thrust through the barred door and injured Collins, and he was captured along with his slave.

Fraser's men would go after another young man who had ties to both Collins and Gordon. Isaac Stow was a miller for Gordon and the nephew of Collins. Stow was home with his wife and their daughter, who was under a year old, when five of Fraser's men captured him. Stow was detained but attempted to run away and notify Gordon of the British attack. It was too late for him to warn Gordon, and it would be too late to save himself, as a Mohawk warrior threw a spear at Stow and struck him in the back before driving a tomahawk into his skull. Stow was scalped and killed, but his wife and daughter were able to escape by wading across the nearby creek and hiding in the woods.

Munro and the commanding officers continued their raid on Ball's Town, targeting specific Americans as they went before setting the town ablaze.

Families were torn asunder at the conclusion of the raid on Ball's Town. In the days after the raid, many of the people of the town gathered at the Ballston fort and slept in the woods near Ballston Lake, as they had lost their homes, crops, livestock and more. Some families were forced to move in with relatives in nearby towns. Others chose to move back to family homes in New England from which they left to settle in Ball's Town. The men who were captured by Munro and Fraser, including Lieutenant Colonel Gordon and other militiamen, were taken as prisoners to Canada, where they would serve their time in Montreal or Quebec until the conclusion of the Revolution.

THE RAIDS UNDER CARLETON would have many social implications for the areas. Due to the raids, crops could not be planted or harvested, grains that had been collected by the New Yorkers were destroyed by the British and their Native allies in the raids and people who were proven to show loyalty to the Continental Congress were taken as prisoners. As a result of these, the American forces feared their armies going hungry with the destruction of stored grains and the inability of the local populaces to plant and harvest their crops. On an even more serious scale, the Americans feared that the frontier raids carried out by Carleton (and others) would lead the citizens of the affected areas to seek protection from the British and that they would switch their loyalties from Patriot or neutral to Loyalists, if only to keep themselves, their families and their livelihoods safe. With the raids continuing in New York, the Sullivan Campaign would be instituted by General George Washington in 1779 to get back at the British. The Sullivan Campaign would be responsible for the burning of Seneca and Mohawk villages in New York and Pennsylvania and would lead the Americans into battle against the forces of famed Mohawk war chief Joseph Brant.

6

THE JESSUP RAIDS

The areas of Kingsbury, Queensbury, Fort Edward and others would experience more than raids over the course of the American Revolution. In Upstate New York, several towns in the Lake George region were born during the 1760s and 1770s and would suffer at the hands of the very barons who purchased the land.

In the mid-1760s, brothers Edward and Ebenezer Jessup moved from Dutchess County, New York, to Albany, New York, and engaged in land speculation in the Hudson River Valley and the Lake George area. The Jessups became friendly with Sir William Johnson, who had built Fort William Henry on the southern end of Lake George during the French and Indian War and who would become the superintendent of Indian affairs after building a close relationship with the Mohawks of New York. The Jessups would purchase much of their land from Johnson and from the Mohawks. Prior to the outbreak of the American Revolution, the Jessup brothers purchased the land that would become the towns of Lake Luzerne, Hadley, Corinth, Warrensburg, Thurman, Chestertown and Johnsburg. With the land, the Jessups built sawmills and rafted logs. They established a community named Jessup's Landing (which today is the Village of Corinth), and they maintained a ferry and a road that followed the river upstream to Jessup's Falls (today, known as Rockwell Falls) between Lake Luzerne and Hadley. The vast landholdings of the Jessups added up to over one million

The Jessup Patent and the surrounding patents. *From* Adirondack Atlas: The Adirondack Almanack and John Warren.

acres of land and would encompass nearly all of what is now northern and western Warren County. With the huge landholdings, the brothers would become the first great lumber barons of the Adirondacks.

The Jessups were successful in the Adirondack region when it came to purchasing land and establishing hamlets, towns and villages, but in the 1770s, when tensions were running high between Loyalists and Patriots, the people began to turn on the Jessups, and in the 1780s, the Jessups turned on the people living on their land. During the winter months of 1775, despite the war not yet having been officially declared, the colonists began to destroy property belonging to the Jessups. The colonists burned the mills and destroyed the ferry. The mils that managed to survive were closed and saw the workers laid off and provisions packed. Much as other Loyalists experienced at this time, the Jessups faced threats of arrest and death and would flee to Canada. Edward and Ebenezer escaped to Canada by snowshoeing up the Sacandaga River and met up with John Johnson and other Loyalists who were also fleeing New York at Fish House in Northampton. From there, the fleeing party continued up the West Branch and over the Long Lake Military Road and onward to Canada.

In the summer of 1776, Sir Guy Carleton was successful in driving American forces out of Quebec, and the Jessups led a party of eighty Loyalists to Crown Point. The Jessup party would become attached to Sir John Johnson's King's Royal Regiment of New York.

In May 1777, Edward Jessup found himself in hot water. On May 6, 1777, Colonel Gordon, who was in command of the Continental Militia in the Ball's Town district, pursued and captured thirty-one Loyalists on or near the Jessup Patent. All thirty-one of those Loyalists admitted that they were on their way to join General John Burgoyne's army and escape taking the oath of allegiance to Congress. Edward Jessup, however, was hotly pursued by Gordon and his militia. To evade capture, Jessup leaped across a gorge in the Hudson where the water was only twelve feet wide.

Jessup then made his way across Queensbury by an old road that ran parallel to the present route from French Mountain to Fort Ann(e). This trail would have taken Jessup over West Mountain and would cross the military trail leading from Fort George to Fort Edward. From Queensbury to Fort Ann(e), Jessup would have sought to camp on high ground above the wetlands in the vicinity of modern-day Route 149. In the Fort Ann(e) area, a stream known as Halfway Brook (because it was halfway between Fort Edward and Fort George) joins Wood Creek leading to Skenesborough (Whitehall). Jessup would then continue northward through Skenesborough to meet with Burgoyne's army encamped at Willsborough Falls. Edward would then join his brother, Ebenezer, who had fled to join Burgoyne some months earlier and had received a commission in Burgoyne's army.

In the summer of 1777, General Gates dispatched militiamen under a Lieutenant Ellis to raid the Jessup Patent. Although the patent had already been thoroughly raided by the Americans, they thought it beneficial to raid anyway. The Loyalist leaders in the Jessup Patent had fled in the previous years, but the militiamen under Lieutenant Ellis destroyed the houses, burned the grain fields and pillaged the Jessup homestead.

As for the Jessup brothers themselves, Lieutenant Colonel Ebenezer and Captain Edward would lead the King's Loyal American Corps in General John Burgoyne's 1777 Campaign. With the goal of capturing the Hudson River via Albany using a multipronged strategy, the 1777 Campaign, known as the Saratoga Campaign, would fail with the October surrender of Burgoyne's army to the American army under General Gates. Both Edward and Ebenezer were among those who surrendered at Saratoga and marched north to Canada.

While in Canada for the winter, the British plan to raid the New York frontier and various key positions came to fruition.

On October 1, 1778, Major Christopher Carleton led a detachment of 800 British Regulars with the Twenty-Ninth Regiment, a company of German levies, 300 Loyalists and 175 Amerindian warriors on raids across New York. Colonel Ebenezer Jessup led the Loyalist battalion, which would act as guides in New York and ensure that no farmhouse, regardless of how isolated from civilization it was, remained unscathed.

In 1779, the Jessup brothers were included among a list of Loyalists who had attained the charge of treason by New York; the consequence of this charge was death should either, or both, of the Jessups be caught by Patriots in New York's borders. The brothers also had all of their property and landholdings seized by the State of New York. With the threat of death, Ebenezer feared for his safety and moved with his family to Ontario. Edward, however, would not flee to Canada once again. In November 1781, Edward Jessup was named major commandant of a new corps of Loyal Rangers. This new corps would be known colloquially as Jessup's Rangers. Jessup's Rangers would be present at the British raid on Ball's Town and would be perpetrators of raids against the settlements in Queensbury, Glens Falls, Kingsbury, Fort Edward and Fort Anne.

Edward Jessup did not play a major role in the raid on Ball's Town, though he and his rangers participated under the command of Major Christopher Carleton. Jessup and his rangers, who were all familiar with the area they were raiding because they had all, at one time, lived in the area, moved with Carleton (in October 1780) south along Lake Champlain past the unmanned Fort Ticonderoga and arrived at Skenesborough on October 8. The following day, Jessup and his rangers moved on the ramshackle and undermanned Fort Anne. The fort was under the command of Captain Adiel Sherwood who, on hearing of Carleton's and Jessup's advance, sent out a scouting party to see what he and his seventy-four men would be up against. This scouting party would not have the chance to return to Captain Sherwood, as they were ambushed by Amerindian warriors under Carleton's command who captured and/or killed most of the men in the party. Jessup's Rangers were present to receive the surrender of Fort Anne and moved on to attack Fort George with Carleton as well. From there, Jessup and his men attacked Kingsbury, Queensbury and Glens Falls by raiding the settlements to the ground. After this raid, Edward Jessup and his men made their way back to Canada, where they engaged in the construction of fortifications in and around Montreal and the lower Lake Champlain region.

In the fall of 1781, Jessup led his own series of raids in Upstate New York. Once again, the Queensbury area would be hit particularly hard. The Oneida hamlet, as Queensbury was once called, was first settled around 1763, after the Seven Years' War ravaged the area. These first settlers established their homesteads around the modern streets of Ridge Road, Glenwood Avenue and Hovey Pond. These first settlers, and those who remained in the area at the time of the American Revolution, were Quakers. Quakers, sometimes known as the Religious Society of Friends, were pacifists; however, despite the Quakers' antiwar leanings, the British believed their farms and homesteads to be threats to their cause to preserve their colonies. Due to the belief that these homes could be used to benefit the Patriot troops in the area, Jessup and his rangers marched on Queensbury and burned the town to the ground a second time. Unfortunately, there is not much information available regarding the Jessup raid on Queensbury. The British records remain spotty, as they did not consider the actions of American-born Loyalists to be on par with those born in Britain, and the Americans did not keep accurate records on the smaller actions the Loyalist troops took against them. Despite the lack of details, this second raid on the area caused people to fear for their lives and leave the area. The destruction of the farmland and cattle led to the limiting of grain and meat, which was detrimental to the armies of both sides of the war and the few families who opted to remain in the area.

In April 1783, with the official conclusion of the American Revolution, Edward Jessup's corps of Loyal Rangers was ordered to disband by the end of December of that year. As for Ebenezer, after the war's end he would unsuccessfully petition for compensation for the property that was lost as a result of his loyal support to the Crown. All of the land the Jessups owned prior to the outbreak of the Revolution was removed from their possession by the government of the State of New York. Like the Jessups, most New York Loyalists who would not take an oath of allegiance to the new American government were dispossessed of their landholdings. However, the Jessups would continue their legacy as land barons in their new lives as citizens of Upper Canada. At the conclusion of the war, Edward and some of his soldiers settled in Canada along the St. Lawrence River, where Jessup would found the town of Prescott around 1810. Jessup and remnants of his rangers were also allotted various townships that would become the towns of Edwardsburg, Augusta, Elizabethtown and Ernestown. In the fall of 1784, Edward Jessup followed in his brother's footsteps and traveled to London, England, to submit his own petition for compensation to recuperate his losses during the American Revolution; like his brother, his petition was unsuccessful.

A historical land marker depicting the site of the Jessup homestead in Lake Luzerne, New York. *Marie D.A. Williams.*

Despite the actions of the brothers, their family name continues to have some prominence in New York. In the town of Lake Luzerne, the site of the first mill established by the Jessups can

Remains of an old bridge located in the Jessup Patent in Lake Luzerne, New York. *Marie D.A. Williams.*

be visited, and in the town of Corinth, the local swimming area is known as Jessup's Landing, the original name for the settlement. The Jessups, particularly Edward, would continue lives of land speculation in Canada. As a military member of rank at the conclusion of the war, Edward was awarded land in the amount of 1,200 acres. He would continue to apply for various land grants and was awarded another 3,800 acres in Ontario as well as a considerable amount of land in Sorel. Jessup also held office as the executive councel of Upper Canada, as a judge of the Court of Common Pleas and as lieutenant colonel of the militias of Edwardsburg, Augusta and Elizabethtown. Jessup was successful in his life, and he saw his son succeed in life as well. After the establishment of the town of Prescott, much of the area, including his own home, was taken over by the army, which built Fort Wellington, a War of 1812 fort, on the property. Edward would pass away shortly after, in February 1816, after having been bedridden for several years.

THE SIR JOHN JOHNSON RAIDS

In 1760, when he was just eighteen years old, John Johnson, the only white son of Sir William Johnson, became the captain of a company of the Tryon County militia. Shortly thereafter, he would leave New York to pursue higher education in England. While studying in England, he was able to enter high society and enter the good graces of King George III, who would bestow Johnson's father's hereditary title on him after having it confirmed, knighting him Sir John Johnson in 1765. With the death of his father in 1774, John Johnson became major general of the Tryon County militia. That milestone was short-lived, however, as he and other Loyalists and Loyalist sympathizers were forced to evacuate New York and flee to Canada to evade arrest by the Patriots in 1776. Once in Canada, Johnson raised the King's Royal Regiment of New York, which comprised men from the Mohawk Valley region who had fled to Canada to avoid arrest.

Johnson participated in the siege of Fort Stanwix and the Battle of Oriskany. However, Johnson would rise to fame for his participation in the raid against Ball's Town and through carrying out his raids in the Mohawk and Schoharie Valleys.

For his part of the raid against Ball's Town, in May 1780, Sir John Johnson led his King's Royal Regiment, along with Loyalists from Major Edward Jessup's King's Loyal Americans, Major Daniel McAlpin's American Volunteers and a sizeable number of Mohawk warriors south from Crown Point. Johnson's fighting force totaled nearly 530 men, and this force made its way to Johnstown, where it scattered a small contingent of Tryon County militiamen on May 21, capturing 27 of the men. Johnson's forces burned 120 barns, mills and houses and gathered about 150 Loyalists before returning to Crown Point.

In 1780, General John Sullivan had been ordered by General and Commander-in-Chief George Washington to pillage Amerindian villages in response to the raids perpetrated by the British. However, in October 1780, the Amerindians sought revenge against Sullivan and his allied Amerindians and planned extensive raids against the Mohawk and Schoharie settlements. Johnson, along with Mohawk war chief Joseph Brant and the famed Cornplanter, led these raids.

The groups met at Tioga Point, where they ascended the Susquehanna Valley and formed a junction at Unadilla with Johnson and his forces. Johnson's fighting force consisted of three companies of Green Dragoons, one company of German Yagers, two hundred of John Butler's rangers, one company of British regulars under Captain Duncan and a sizeable number of Mohawk warriors. Johnson's force came from Oswego by way of Montreal with a plan to invade Schenectady. The plan was to move along the Charlotte River to its source, cross to the head of the Schoharie, devastate all of the settlements along its course until its junction with the Mohawk was reached and then weave a path of destruction down the Mohawk Valley and into Schenectady. The raid was successful in how much devastation was caused but failed in that the forces did not sack Schenectady.

Johnson and his forces moved from Fort Hunter on the Mohawk River on October 17 and destroyed everything in their path. On October 18, Johnson began his march up the Mohawk Valley, where settlements at Caughnawaga were burned along with settlements on both sides of the river as far west as Fort Plain. Johnson's men singled out a man named Jelles Fonda to suffer destruction to his home. Fonda had been an officer under Johnson but abandoned the British cause. As revenge for his leaving the British army, his mansion was burned along with property estimated at $60,000 in the town of Palatine. Fonda was not present at the time, and his wife was able to escape to Schenectady.

Johnson and his men encamped in Palatine on October 18 and moved to the north side at Keder's Riff (Spraker's Basin) the following day. A large part of the army continued up the river to destroy crops and buildings while another detachment was sent to a small stockade named Fort Paris in Stone Arabia located about two and a half miles from the Mohawk River. Fort Paris was located close to the hamlet at Stone Arabia and was occupied by a Colonel John Brown with a garrison of 130 men. Word had

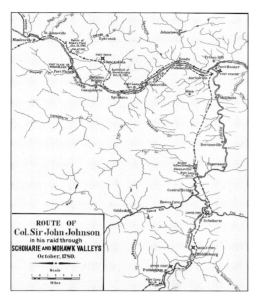

Sir John Johnson's series of raids. *James A. Roberts, New York State Archives.*

been sent to Albany about Johnson's intent to attack the fort. On hearing of the movements of the British in the Mohawk and Schoharie Valleys, General Robert Van Rensselaer, with regiments from Claverack, Albany and Schenectady, pushed on to encounter Johnson's men. The prior evening, on October 17, Rensselaer's men were encamped on a farm in Florida, near the present-day city of Amsterdam. Rensselaer heard that Johnson's men were advancing and sent word to Colonel Brown and his troops to check on Johnson's advance, preparing his own men to fall to the rear of the American forces. Brown marched halfway toward the river and, on October 19, engaged in battle with Sir John Johnson's troops. Johnson had diverted a large part of his forces to engage with Rensselaer at the rear of the American advance, preventing the Americans from successfully defending Fort Paris and Stone Arabia. Brown was overpowered by the British forces, but they continued fighting while slowly making a retreat. While making a retreat from the field, Brown sustained a musket ball to the chest and died instantly.

Johnson then dispersed his forces as small bands to various locations in a six-mile radius to pillage the countryside. Johnson's men decimated Stone Arabia and made their way to Klock's farm near the present-day village of St. Johnsville. General Van Rensselaer was in proximity to Johnson's army with a fighting force of 1,500 soldiers, volunteers and Oneida warriors led by Louis Atayataronghta. These forces outnumbered those of Johnson. Van Rensselaer's forces caught up with Johnson's forces at Klock's farm and

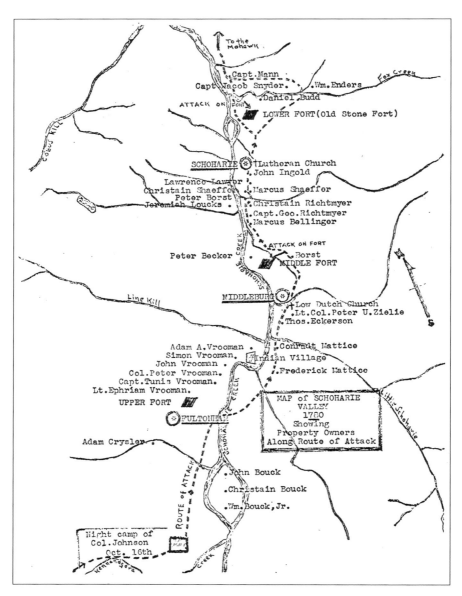

Sir John Johnson's Schoharie raid, including towns and landowners along the route of attack. *Brown/Wheeler Family History blog.*

engaged in battle that resulted in Johnson's men losing the field as darkness fell. Johnson's men had boats hidden on nearby Onondaga Lake; they raced to the boats, beating the pursuing Americans, and headed back to Oswego. As Johnson's men made their escape, they destroyed two valleys at low casualty rates to their own forces—nine killed, two wounded and fifty-three missing. Johnson continued to lay waste to the Mohawk and Schoharie Valleys in the remaining months of 1780, burning large quantities of grain and flour intended for use by the Continental army.

THE YEAR 1782 BROUGHT great changes for Sir John Johnson. The first half of the year saw Johnson appointed as brigadier general and as "Superintendent General and Inspector General of the Six Nations Indians and those in Province of Quebec." He took over this role from his cousin Guy Johnson, who had been discovered falsifying his war reports. Johnson, like his father before him, championed the causes of the Amerindians under his care and never failed to demonstrate his concern for their well-being, interests and rights.

After the war's end, Johnson was appointed by Governor Frederick Haldimand to supervise the settlement of Loyalist refugees who had fled New York for upper St. Lawrence and the Bay of Quinte. Beginning in 1784 and for many years after, the people of those settlements regarded Johnson as their leader. He petitioned on their behalf to the king so that the settlements might enjoy freehold tenure of lands under English civil law in 1785, and in 1791, when Upper Canada was created, it was expected by the people that Johnson would be awarded its first lieutenant governor; however, that position would be awarded to John Graves Simcoe, who had experienced the Revolution on Long Island. Disappointed with not being granted the position, Johnson moved his family to London for four years but found his abilities went unappreciated and returned to Canada.

In the fall of 1796, Johnson and his family moved to Montreal, where he was appointed to the Legislative Council of Lower Canada and resumed his duties as the head of the Department of Indian Affairs for Lower Canada. In this position, Johnson continued to provide the Amerindians with their needs and champion their rights and best interests.

Johnson would be a landowner of property in both Upper and Lower Canada and would live a long life dedicated to his Amerindian allies. He died at the age of eighty-eight in Montreal in the year 1830, still as the head of the Department of Indian Affairs.

8

THE JOSEPH BRANT RAIDS

Joseph Brant, leader of the Mohawks, was the brother-in-law of Sir William Johnson and harbored pro-British tendencies due to the good relations between the British and the Mohawks. The threat of revolution would bring a period of instability to the Iroquois as it would to white Americans and African Americans. The Iroquois, as a collective and as individual tribes, wanted to side with those they believed would benefit the Confederacy. For the Mohawks in particular, the British were seen as the right people to side with. Prior to the outbreak of the Revolution, Sir William John and his only white son, Sir John Johnson, befriended the Mohawks in New York and maintained strong relationships with the tribe. Also prior to the outbreak of the Revolution, and as a direct response to the French and Indian War, the British instituted the Proclamation of 1763 to prevent the further encroachment on lands designated for the various Native American peoples in America. These actions prompted the Mohawks to take the side of the British during the Revolution because the Mohawks believed that the British had their best interests in mind, whereas the Patriots disagreed with the validity of the Proclamation of 1763 and thus did not have the best interests of the various Native American tribes in mind.

Chief Joseph Brant, or Thayendanegea, took up arms for the British in the outbreak of the revolution. He led an army of Mohawk and Seneca warriors, who would conduct raids throughout New York State. At the surrender of the British at Saratoga, Brant's warriors frequently conducted raids around the state, beginning in 1778. For Brant, the loss of the British at Saratoga was a devastating blow, and it was one that meant the Mohawks, Senecas and other Native American tribes were in danger. Brant applied to work with Captain John Butler, who would carry out raids in New York with Brant. The first of these raids was the Cherry Valley Raid, known also as the Cherry Valley Massacre (described earlier in this chapter). The goal of the Cherry Valley Raid, and of other raids that would be carried out by Brant, was not merely to destroy areas with a great Patriot-leaning presence but also to gather much-needed supplies and Loyalist soldiers for the British military, and Brant was successful in achieving that goal.

One of the first raids that Joseph Brant participated in after the 1777 British surrender at Saratoga was the Battle of Cobleskill, also known as the Cobleskill Massacre. Months prior to the battle, in February 1778, Joseph Brant established his base of operations at Onaquaga, present-day Windsor, New York, where he recruited a mixed battalion of both Iroquois warriors and Loyalists. This fighting force numbered between two hundred and three hundred men by the time Brant began his campaign to raid a number of settlements on New York's frontier in May of that year. Like the raids led by Sir John Johnson, Major Christopher Carleton and Major Edward Jessup, one of the objectives Brant had for his raiding campaign was to secure provisions for both his fighting force and the fighting force of John Butler, who would lead a raiding campaign in the Susquehanna River Valley on the New York and Pennsylvania border.

At the time of the raid, the settlement of Cobleskill consisted of only twenty families who lived on farms spread along Cobleskill Creek. The area, a part of the Schoharie Creek region, was a major source of food and other supplies for the American war effort. Unfortunately for the settlement of Cobleskill, its only defense from attack was a small local militia under the command of Captain Christian Brown. For some time, rumors of attacks by Iroquois warriors had made their way to the settlement. Christian Brown appealed to the Continental army for additional men to help defend the settlement from the impending attack. Around forty men from the Seventh Massachusetts Regiment, under the command of Captain William Patrick, were sent to Cobleskill to reinforce the local militia.

On May 30, 1778, Brant's attack on Cobleskill began. In the early morning hours, Brant laid a trap for the Americans defending the settlement—he sent a small number of his warriors out as a lure, and Captain Patrick and his forces took the bait, noticing the few Iroquois warriors near the southern edge of the Cobleskill settlement. Captain Brown made an attempt to warn Captain Patrick that the Iroquois forces at the southern edge of the settlement might be setting a trap, but Captain Patrick and his men moved to engage the Iroquois warriors nonetheless, engaging them in a running battle that would lead directly to Brant's larger force and his death, along with the death of his lieutenant and about half of his men. Knowing that the local militia would not be able to fend off Brant's forces, Captain Brown ordered a retreat. On their retreat, Brown's force made its way to Fort Clinton; however, five of Brown's men sought refuge in a house owned by a man named George Warner—an action that would lead to their deaths, as some of Brant's warriors set the house on fire. Brant and his fighting force burned down ten houses and an unknown number of other buildings, raided the farms for supplies and killed any cattle they could not take with them before withdrawing. The Battle of Cobleskill had a high casualty rate compared to the number of belligerents involved; Brant's fighting force suffered an estimated twenty-five casualties compared to its two to three hundred fighters and the Americans suffered twenty-two slain settlers, eight wounded and five captured compared to its fighting force of around sixty men between the forces under Captain Patrick and Captain Brown.

The harsh treatment under Brant and his raiding force was not yet finished. The five prisoners taken by Brant's men were going to suffer death by being burned alive at the stake, with Brant and his warriors going so far as to make the prisoners gather the wood themselves. The fire was started, and before they could be sent to their deaths, one of the prisoners, Lieutenant Maynard, gave the Freemason signal for distress. Brant, a Freemason himself, noticed Maynard giving the signal and put a stop to the deaths of the prisoners. Instead, the prisoners were forced to march for forty days to Quebec (but first made a stop in Montreal), in which the only sources of food and water were what they found along the way. When they arrived in Quebec, the prisoners were ransomed by the British authorities and would remain prisoners of war until the war's end in 1783, with the signing of the Treaty of Paris.

Brant and his men would continue to march throughout the Upstate New York region and would continue to raid various settlements in the frontier region. In September 1778, Brant and his men conducted a raid on German Flatts in modern-day Herkimer County.

The settlement of German Flatts (now known as Herkimer) was established in 1723 by Palatine German immigrants. Like Cobleskill, the settlement was defended by local militia, in this case under the command of Colonel Peter Bellinger, and there were two forts in the area—Fort Dayton and Fort Herkimer.

Brant had planned to raid German Flatts earlier than September and made his plans known to the survivors of the smaller raids; however, he was unable to do so because he planned on having John Butler and Butler's Rangers to raid with him. By early September, it became increasingly obvious to Brant that Butler was not going to be able to join him, so Brant and Captain William Caldwell launched the raid with the men they had.

After receiving warnings that Brant was going to attack the German Flatts area, Colonel Bellinger of the local militia made it a point to send scouts near Brant's base of operations at Unadilla to gather intelligence on his movements. On September 16, Brant's company attacked one of Bellinger's scouting parties, killing a few of the men, while the others scattered. One of the survivors who ran off after the engagement managed to get twenty-six miles ahead of Brant's advance and warned the people of the German Flatts settlement. After receiving the warning, Colonel Bellinger enlisted the help of Colonel Jacob Klock and his regiment, while the settlers of German Flatts took refuge in the area forts.

The warning the settlers received about the impending attack by Joseph Brant and his mixed force of raiders would become a bit of a benefit to the settlers. During the raid, because the people took refuge in the forts,

The farms that were affected by the Cherry Valley Massacre in November 1778. *Reverend H.V. Swinnerton, State Historical Society of Wisconsin.*

Brant and his raiders were unable to take prisoners and/or scalps. They also lacked the necessary heavy weaponry to lay siege on the forts and instead had to resort to rampaging through the settlements on both sides of the Mohawk River. Brant's forces were able to drive off a sizeable amount of barnyard and labor animals and were able to destroy nearly sixty-five homes and barns, three gristmills and a sawmill. More than seven hundred people at German Flatts were made homeless due to the destruction caused by Brant and his forces. In the end, the only buildings that remained unmolested by Brant were the forts, a church and homes belonging to the Loyalists in the area.

The raid on German Flatts did not just anger the people of the settlement. With Brant's absence from Unadilla, the Iroquois who had not sided with the British, namely the Oneida and the Tuscarora, took the opportunity to raid Unadilla and freed many of the prisoners Brant had taken during his raids. American forces then launched their own raids in early October as retaliation against the British raids. In these, Unadilla and Onaquaga would be destroyed. As retaliation against the Americans' retaliation, Joseph Brant and Walter Butler, the son of John Butler, launched a raiding expedition against the settlement of Cherry Valley, an important settlement in the Schoharie Valley, which would be the scene of a massacre and would cause Brant to experience loss, grief and regret.

Raid on Cherry Valley

After the attack on German Flatts, the combined forces of Joseph Brant and Captain Walter Butler moved to attack the Cherry Valley settlement in the Schoharie Valley. Under Brant were his Iroquois warriors and Loyalist troops. Under Butler were two companies of Butler's Rangers commanded by Captain William Caldwell and John McDonell, fifty soldiers from the Eighth Regiment of Foot, and three hundred Senecas led by either Cornplanter or Sayenqueraghta (historians remain unsure). Cherry Valley was located in modern-day Otsego County, about seventy miles east of Albany, and was protected by a palisade that was built after Brant's raid on Cobleskill.

On November 11, 1778, Colonel Ichabod Alden, who had been put in charge of the soldiers at the fort at Cherry Valley, ignored intelligence about a hostile force of British soldiers and Native American warriors. This would prove to be devastating for those who were stationed at the fort and who lived in the town of Cherry Valley.

In the early morning hours of November 11, the fighting began, caused by some overeager Native Americans who fired on a group of settlers. The settlers sounded the alarm that Cherry Valley was under attack. The raid that was carried out devastated the area and would be referred to by Americans as a massacre for good reason; out of a fighting force of around 250 Americans and an unknown number of villagers in the area, the Americans sustained 44 deaths with 70 initial captures, mostly women and children, though around 30 of those captured were returned. The village was destroyed—not a single structure stood at the raid's conclusion. The battle was seen as a massacre not merely because of the amount of life that was lost on the side of the Americans but also because of the inability of Brant and Butler to control a band of Seneca warriors. The Senecas ignored a request during a war council prior to the battle, which involved Brant and Butler stating that noncombatants were not to be harmed. As a result, deaths of those in the area who had Loyalist sympathies, many of whom Brant had considered friends, occured at the hands of the Senecas.

In the rural frontier regions of New York, nothing struck fear into the souls of the people, regardless of their sympathies at the time of the Revolution, like Indian raids. The devastation of Cherry Valley would prompt General Washington and Congress to usher in the Sullivan Expedition, which was a force of Continental soldiers under the leadership of John Sullivan that conducted raids on Mohawk and Seneca villages beginning in 1779 as a countermeasure against Brant and Butler, who would continue to carry out raids in New York—an expedition that would be known as the Great Burning of the Valleys. The various raids carried out by Brant brought death and destruction in their wake, with the sole purpose of ensuring that there were supplies for the British forces but not for the American forces. As Brant's raids continued, and as other Loyalists carried out raids in New York, many New Yorkers left their settlements for areas farther south that were not affected by Indian raids or by the Revolution in general. This would lead to a major decrease in the population of the frontier lands but would not lead to the end of the raids as the Revolution continued to rage on in New York.

Raid on Canajoharie and Fort Plain

After the attack on Cherry Valley by Joseph Brant and others in November 1780, considered the worst attack of the year and prompting Congress to act against the Native American tribes who had sided with the British during the war, the forces of Joseph Brant, Sir John Johnson and Walter Butler continued to pillage and plunder the frontier regions of New York. Among the many areas the Loyalists would attack in their campaign, known widely as the Burning of the Valleys, were Canajoharie and Fort Plain in August 1780.

In Canajoharie, the primary fortification was Fort Plank. Described as a three-story blockhouse surrounded by earthworks, Fort Plank was located on a plain overlooking the village of Fort Plain. Prior to the August attacks on the area, Fort Plank was occupied by Colonel Peter Gansevoort's American regiment with the duty of escorting and relocating supplies to Fort Stanwix (also known as Fort Schuyler, which played a role in the Battle of Oriskany during the 1777 Saratoga Campaign). Knowing the Americans planned to move the supplies to Fort Stanwix in early August 1780, Joseph Brant spread rumors that he was planning to attack the supply convoy as well as Fort Stanwix. As a result of these rumors, Brant and his forces were able to enter Canajoharie unopposed. They were successful in destroying over fifty homes, over fifty barns, a mill and a church. Brant and his men also killed sixteen inhabitants who had not fled with others to nearby Forts Plank, Clyde or other strongholds in the area and managed

A historical land marker depicting the location of the Battle of Stone Arabia. *Mohawk Valley History.*

to capture about fifty other people. Brant and his forces also killed (or took) an estimated three hundred head of cattle. Much like his other raids, the primary objective was to destroy the settlements and secure any goods that were intended for use by American troops. Due to this primary objective, Brant did not waste any time in attacking the forts around Canajoharie and instead moved on to another area.

There were two supposed reasons for why Brant did not attack Fort Plain when he had the opportunity to do so: his mother was from the area, and although he wanted to cause harm for the Americans in the area, he did not want to completely decimate the area his mother was from, and because the fort's garrison was away escorting supplies to Fort Stanwix, women and children in the area had fled to Fort Plain (and Fort Clyde, as previously mentioned) and dressed in men's uniforms, walked the ramparts of the fort and gave Brant's forces the impression that the fort was still heavily garrisoned and thus would put up a strong defense. According to information provided by the Fort Plain Museum, the impromptu plan worked, as Brant did not attack the fort and more people were saved than harmed and killed.

The Battle of Stone Arabia/Klock's Field

On the morning of October 19, 1780, the forces of Sir John Johnson and Joseph Brant, consisting of the Eighth Regiment of Foot, the Thirty-Fourth Regiment, Butler's Rangers, the King's Royal Regiment of New York, Iroquois warriors and Yager Riflemen, crossed the Mohawk River at Anthony's Nose (in the north end of Westchester County) and moved up the river.

Under Brant's command, some of his warriors went ahead and burned some buildings near Fort Frey in search of plunder. At nearby Fort Paris in Stone Arabia, Colonel John Brown heard about the attacks and ordered a detachment of levies to join the Albany County militia under Robert Van Rensselaer. The groups would pursue the Loyalist forces in a running battle.

That morning, Colonel Brown marched out of Fort Paris with about 340 men from the Tryon County militia, New York and Massachusetts levies and rangers and went toward the Mohawk River, unaware that the Loyalist forces were much closer than he expected.

In the distance, Johnson and some of his men saw horsemen watching their movements. Brant and some of his warriors pursued the horsemen as they made their retreat to Stone Arabia. The horsemen led the Iroquois warriors right to the American advance guard under the command of Major Oliver Root, and the advanced guard was surprised and retreated back to Brown's main body. Brant and his warriors hotly pursued Root's advance guard and found themselves vastly outnumbered by the American forces. However, at the same time, Johnson's detachment was able to gain the heights of Stone Arabia, where Johnson saw Brant's warriors making a hasty retreat from Root's forces, and Johnson made the decision to advance with his Eighth and Thirty-Fourth Regiments as well as his Butler's Rangers to reinforce Brant. With this decision, the American forces were outnumbered and overwhelmed.

Colonel Brown and his men fought bravely but were ultimately no match for the British forces. While hiding behind some trees, Brown was hit by a musket ball in the chest and died instantly. Root then took command of the American forces.

As he observed the fighting, Johnson saw Brant's warriors outflanking the Americans on the left and ordered Butler's Rangers to attack the Americans on the right while he, leading the Eighth and Thirty-Fourth Regiments, attacked the American center. The fight was brutal, with many of Brown's detachments killed or wounded and the Americans retreating in a disorganized manner. As Brown's/Root's men retreated from the field, Brant's warriors scalped the Americans who were dead and dying on the field. On examining Brown's body, several letters were found on his person stating that Major General Robert Van Rensselaer was at Fort Hunter with about six hundred men. Johnson made the decision that rather than engaging Van Rensselaer's forces, the Loyalists would make their way to Oneida Lake, where they had boats and provisions hidden. However, in the evening of October 19, Van Rensselaer, who commanded units from the Albany County militia, along with New York levies under the command of Colonels John Harper and Lewis DuBois, chased Johnson and Brant to an area known as Klock's Field in modern-day St. Johnsville.

On Klock's Field, a running battle between Van Rensselaer's American forces and Johnson's Loyalist forces occurred. Johnson's men were outflanked on the left side by Van Rensselaer's men. Despite this, it would become apparent to Van Rensselaer that his right and left flanks were actually firing on each other. Van Rensselaer ordered a cease-fire so his men could retreat to the Klock farmhouse for rest. Knowing that Van Rensselaer had ordered a temporary cease-fire and retreat, Johnson and Brant took the opportunity to cross the Mohawk River at King Hendrick's Ford (to avoid either Fort House on East Canada Creek or Fort Windecker). During this escape,

Johnson and Brant's men were forced to abandon their possessions—the baggage, cannons and even prisoners they had captured along the way—to make their hasty escape from Van Rensselaer's forces. The men were able to retreat under the cover of darkness across the Mohawk River. After several grueling days of travel, the Loyalist forces were successful in making their way to Fort Oswego on October 27, 1780.

Although it was ultimately the Loyalist forces who were driven from the field and the Americans who would claim victory for this encounter, the Americans suffered greatly for their participation in the Battle of Stone Arabia and Klock's Field. Of Brown's men, there were thirty-six killed (including Brown himself), two who were taken prisoner by the Loyalists and about twelve who were wounded in the battle. The forces of Johnson and Brant, on the other hand, suffered only four men killed and another four men wounded in the battle, including Brant, who injured his foot in the fighting. Despite the mutual retreat, Johnson and Brant were able to achieve the combined goal of their raids by destroying a twenty-mile swath of land from Fort Hunter to Stone Arabia. Under the combined forces of Sir John Johnson and Joseph Brant at Stone Arabia, the Americans suffered greatly for their attacks on Unadilla and Onaquaga.

The Battle of Stone Arabia/Klock's Field was the last major raid that Brant and his warriors would participate in during the American Revolution in New York. For his participation in the various raids, and for the raids he perpetrated on his own, Joseph Brant earned the nickname "Monster Brant" from both Patriot rebels and Loyalists alike. The atrocities carried out by Brant's warriors were said to have damaged American/British/Iroquois relations for half a century after the conclusion of the American Revolution. However, important American figures, such as Colonel Ichabod Alden and Colonel William Stacy (both of whom were Patriots and were present during the raid at Cherry Valley), claimed that Brant was a compassionate leader and showed great restraint during times of chaos and violence, especially toward noncombatants, such as women and children.

After the war's end, as early as 1783, Brant made an appeal to Canadian governor Sir Frederick Haldimand to set aside land for a Mohawk reserve in Ontario. Brant also put the interests of his own people, the Native Americans, above the interests of both the American and British governments. He worked tirelessly as a negotiator between various Native nations and between the three aforementioned groups. In the summer of 1783, Brant initiated the formation of the Western Confederacy, where the Iroquois and twenty-nine other Native nations agreed to defend the Fort Stanwix

Treaty line. However, this would prove difficult as the Americans attacked the Western Confederacy in the Northwest Indian War. The war was a back-and-forth for land between the Western Confederation and the Americans, with Brant acting as a sort of liaison, as he refused to enter the Six Nations as combatants but did not want to leave the Western Confederacy completely defenseless. Brant was semi-successful in securing arms and provisions for the Confederacy from the British government in Quebec. (Semi-successful because the aid arrived in 1794, four years after it was requested.)

Throughout the remainder of his life, Brant worked tirelessly to ensure safety and security for the Six Nations of the Iroquois by working with various governments—the British, French and Americans—to secure tracts of land to serve as a refuge for the Native nations. In the early 1800s, Canadian governor John Graves Simcoe bought a sizeable tract of land on Lake Ontario and gifted it to Joseph Brant. Brant moved onto the property and constructed a home that was a half-scale model of Johnson Hall, where he had lived for a time as a young man. In 1807, Brant passed away in his home, and his remains were laid to rest at a tomb in Her Majesty's Chapel of the Mohawks in Brantford, Ontario.

THE SULLIVAN CAMPAIGN IN WESTERN NEW YORK

The British/Loyalist raids on the frontier lands of New York struck fear in the people of the state due to their unpredictability and the utter devastation they wrought. The Patriots in the area hoped for the Continental army to help them, as their small local militias were unable to stop the carnage. Together with the British/Loyalist forces under Joseph Brant, Sir John Johnson and Christopher Carleton, the Iroquois (with the exception of the Oneida and the Tuscarora) ravaged northern Pennsylvania and various areas around New York, including its Upstate frontier region.

On June 11, 1778, after months of listening to the requests for protection and redress from the people of the settlements that were raided by the Mohawks and Senecas, who sympathized with the British, the Continental Congress declared that an expedition should be undertaken for the purpose of reprimanding hostile Native Americans. Despite the Continental Congress's declaration, actions were not put in place right away. Congress and the Continental army were lacking in money and resources, so the expedition against the Mohawks and Senecas was put on hold until 1779. In early 1779, after the Iroquois and Loyalists attacked the Wyoming Valley settlement in Pennsylvania and the Cherry Valley settlement in New York, commander-in-chief of the Continental army general George Washington wanted to go on the offensive against the Iroquois to punish them for their choice to openly side with the Crown. Washington issued a military campaign to break the Iroquois Confederacy. Called the Sullivan-Clinton Campaign, but often just referred to as the

Sullivan Campaign, this military action struck Iroquois settlements in Pennsylvania and New York. Washington hoped that a quick raid in the Iroquois New York homelands would eliminate (or at least vastly weaken) an essential British ally without burdening his own forces outside New York. Washington sought an experienced commanding officer to lead the charge, but after several officers declined, including General Gates, General John Sullivan of New Hampshire was chosen for the position with assistance from Generals James Clinton, Enoch Poor and William Maxwell. The plan Washington had for the Revolution as a whole was to remain on the defense, unless measures were needed to hold the Mohawks and Senecas in check, which was the case for this campaign. In a letter to Governor Clinton and General Gates, Washington stated that he was determined to hit the Six Nations of the Iroquois where they would feel it the hardest—by attacking their settlements, destroying their crops and wreaking havoc just as the Native Americans had done to the settlements in New York and Pennsylvania.

In May 1779, before the expedition began, Washington wrote a letter to Sullivan explaining the terms of his upcoming expedition. In the letter, Washington explained that the goal of the campaign was the complete destruction of hostile tribes and the capture of "as many persons of every age and sex as possible." The letter also explained who commanded the brigades that would be granted to Sullivan and the path he should take to conquer the hostile Natives. Sullivan agreed with Washington's goals, believing that if his men could destroy the Iroquois food supply and other necessities, it would force the British to provide for the Iroquois throughout the following winter and possibly the remainder of the war, creating a heavy burden on the British.

Sullivan conducted his raids primarily in western and southern New York, even going so far as to attack Mohawk and Seneca villages in Pennsylvania. With four brigades under his command and the command of the aforementioned commanding officers, the men of the Sullivan Campaign numbered 4,500. There was a logistical trial when it came to the feeding, outfitting, paying and general care of these men. As they operated outside the traditional supply lines, Washington had to promise that for the several weeks the campaign was enacted, Sullivan would have his complete support but would have to be self-sufficient.

The plan for the Sullivan Campaign was relatively simple: beginning in Pennsylvania, Sullivan would gather his fighting force near Easton, where they would move up the Susquehanna River Valley. At the same time, the

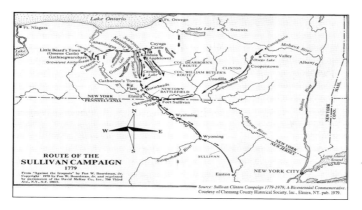

The movements of the Sullivan Campaign and the Battle of Newtown. *Jamestown Settlement & American Revolution Museum at Yorktown.*

fighting force under Clinton's command would make a wide sweep westward from New York's Mohawk Valley to the upper Susquehanna Valley and would join with more forces. General James Clinton would lead a raid against the Onondaga and Oneida in Tioga (near Owego) in conjunction with Colonel Van Schaick. They were told to destroy the villages and fields of those tribes and to destroy everything in their path. However, Washington's goal for the campaign was not just destruction but annihilation. Washington had told Sullivan not to accept any offer of peace before the complete and total destruction of the Iroquois homelands. He wanted the villages burned, the crops destroyed, as many people taken prisoner as possible, and he did not want Sullivan and his men to spare anyone the bayonet if the option to kill was available. Sullivan, per Washington's instruction, would send out small parties to destroy villages that were outside the primary area the Americans would be attacking.

Between the four brigades the Americans had for the expedition, there was a fighting force of nearly five thousand, and the British, who were skeptical about the size of the American force, could only muster a fighting force of about six hundred to go up against the American forces. Knowing they would not be able to face the Americans head-on, the British, under Colonel John Butler, and their Iroquois allies planned to ambush the Sullivan expedition. This encounter would be known as the Battle of Newtown, and it would be the most significant event of the Sullivan Campaign, as it marked a defensive stand against the British-Iroquois forces as opposed to an offensive stand and would lead to an American victory. The victory at this battle led to an increase in American morale, and the expedition would continue throughout 1779.

TIOGA

General Washington had hoped that Sullivan's campaign into Iroquois country would begin a couple of weeks after it was established that Sullivan would be its primary commanding officer, especially given the nature of the raiding parties to travel light without a significant amount of supplies. Sullivan, however, continued to wait until he had all necessary supplies to ensure his men would be well fed and taken care of, even though supplies were low for the Continental army as a whole. Washington continually sent letters to Sullivan to convince him to move his troops and to begin his campaign. By the time Washington dispatched his last letter to Sullivan in July 1779, however, the general was already on the move to link up with Clinton's brigade at Tioga.

Sullivan's delayed advance, although trying the patience of Washington, proved to be beneficial to the campaign. Colonel Daniel Broadhand organized a small force to assist Sullivan by raiding areas northward, beginning at Fort Pitt and moving along the Allegheny River, where they would later combine forces with Sullivan.

Once Sullivan and his forces were nearing Tioga on the convergence of the Cayuga and Susquehanna Rivers, Sullivan sent a scouting party to the village of Chemung, which was located above Tioga. The scouts, on their return to Sullivan, reported that there were between two hundred and three hundred Iroquois in the vicinity of the fort, but they were unsure whether the Iroquois were moving to defend the fort or to evacuate the fort. Although the information he received was questionable at best, Sullivan made the decision to march under the cover of darkness and surprise the town.

On entering Chemung, the American forces found it deserted and took the opportunity to loot the homes for valuables before burning the village to the ground. A brigade under the command of General Edward Hand was able to locate the Iroquois, follow them on their march and engage with them in a skirmish. Although the fight ended quickly, the shooting between the Iroquois and the Americans heightened tensions. Fighting broke out in one of the fields where they were located, American soldiers were wounded and killed and the Americans returned to the Tioga area.

Sullivan waited in Tioga to connect with Clinton's fighting force, but Clinton had already been in Iroquois country near Lake Otsego for a few weeks. Sullivan sent General Hand's forces, around 900 men, to connect with Clinton's forces. As Hand's forces and Sullivan's forces moved through the territory to meet Clinton's men, they burned villages and large swaths of land in two columns. Clinton and Sullivan were able to connect, bringing Sullivan's total fighting force to around 4,500 men—its full strength for the duration of the campaign.

As Sullivan's men camped in August 1779, their camp was surrounded by a handful of Iroquois warriors who sniped them from around the camp's perimeter. Sullivan's response to these attacks was to have his men clear the brush and other forest debris, pushing the camp's perimeter back more than one hundred yards and increasing security patrols. These efforts were unsuccessful as an Iroquois party attacked the camp, killing and scalping one person and attacking the cattle before Sullivan's men drove them off.

Sullivan's men left Tioga on August 26, more than two months after they were supposed to embark on their campaign. The British forces were alerted to the American march and to the strength of their forces and planned to ambush the Americans at the village of Newtown near modern-day Elmira, New York. Captain John Butler and Chief Joseph Brant gathered a force of about seven hundred, which included three hundred of Butler's Rangers. The British used the outline of the land to their advantage against the Americans, constructing a breastwork and camouflaging it with brush and other forest debris in hopes that Sullivan would be drawn across it and would become confused so the British may fire from one flank and then the other.

From these moments, the British and the Americans would become engaged in the Battle of Newtown.

THE BATTLE OF NEWTOWN

The Sullivan Campaign brought about many skirmishes and battles as four brigades roamed the frontier lands of New York and Pennsylvania to conduct raids against the Iroquois, particularly the Mohawks and Seneca, who had chosen to side with the British during the American Revolution instead of remaining neutral or siding with the Americans. Under Joseph Brant, the Mohawks and Seneca conducted raids against various areas in the wilderness, which would have a devastating effect on the societies in those areas. As a result of the British-Iroquois raids, the Americans began conducting their own raids against Iroquois villages, known as the Sullivan Campaign, as the main leader was General John Sullivan. As both Brant and Sullivan wandered the states of New York and Pennsylvania, it was only a matter of time before the two fighting forces would meet on the battlefield. In August 1779, in the town of Newtown, the two forces met.

The goal of the Sullivan Campaign was to attack the villages of Native Americans they deemed as being hostile to the American cause and destroying crops and supplies that could aid the British and the Iroquois warriors. The goal of the British-led Brant Campaign was to attack American villages deemed as being hostile to the British cause and to destroy crops and supplies that could aid the Americans and their allies during the war. With similar goals driving the forces, the campaigns crossed over New York and Pennsylvania numerous times, but it was not until August 29, 1779, that the forces would meet. According to the *Annals of Tryon County*, the Brant Campaign was given intelligence about where the American forces were, and they planned to ambush them. The forces of Brant came to an estimated 1,100 men, and the forces of the Sullivan Campaign dwarfed the Brant Campaign with an estimated force of nearly 5,000. As both forces were going toward the same area—the Americans to raid the villages surrounding Newtown and the British to cut off the Americans—the Americans were successful in raiding some of the villages, such as Chemung, in the last days of August.

As the American forces moved toward Newtown, they were ambushed by a combined force of British and Native American troops. According to staff at the Fort Stanwix National Monument:

On the afternoon of August 29, Sullivan's troops approached the ambush site. Unfortunately for the Indians, the Americans knew a large body of the enemy was nearby and they were being particularly cautious and vigilant. Their advance parties spotted the hidden breastworks and sent back word to the main force. Sullivan determined to occupy the Indians in front of their breastworks with a mixed force of infantry and artillery, while the New Hampshire and New York troops encircled the ridge. Colonel Butler surmised the Americans' plans early on and once again urged the Indians to retreat, but they steadfastly refused to budge. The Indians' resolve was soon shaken as artillery rounds began to fall around them. As the American attack intensified, the Indians and their British allies were forced to retreat from their positions. Mortar shells bursting in the rear of their lines convinced many Indians that they were already encircled, and panic began to spread through their numbers. Luckily for the Indians, the Americans' flanking column had been slowed down in crossing a creek and a swamp. Thus, the main body of the Indians and their allies were able to escape just ahead of the noose that was tightening around them. With their retreat, the Battle of Newtown came to an end. While the Americans did inflict a considerable amount of casualties amongst the Indian forces, their true victory was in totally overpowering the Indians and completely destroying their morale. For the remainder of the campaign, the Americans would be unhindered in their destructive advance.

The Battle of Newtown was merely the beginning of the Sullivan Campaign. Throughout the month of September 1779, Sullivan would lead his army on a destructive path throughout western New York and its Finger Lakes region, destroying Native villages and food stores.

After the American victory at the Battle of Newtown, Sullivan and his army continued to penetrate the First Nations territory, conducting raids in the areas of modern-day Romulus, Canandaigua, Richmond and Geneseo, affecting the modern counties of Seneca County, Ontario County, Livingston County and Genesee County. According to General Sullivan's accounts, more than forty Iroquois villages had been raided, including the villages of Kendaia, Canadaigua, Honeoye, Geneseo, Catharine's Town, Goiogouen, Chonodote and Kanadaseaga. Crops and livestock belonging to the Iroquois had been destroyed, and in late September 1779, the Mohawk population would be dispossessed of their landholdings in the state.

TEANTONTALAGO

The last days of September 1779 would see the final actions of the Sullivan Campaign. On September 27, a fraction of General James Clinton's brigade, under the command of Colonel Peter Gansevoort of the Third New York Regiment, was sent toward Fort Stanwix to its winter quarters. However, the detachment stopped at Teantontalago, near modern-day Schenectady, and carried out orders to arrest and detain every Mohawk male in Albany until 1780, when they were released.

The action taken at Teantontalago effectively dispossessed the Mohawks of their land in the Hudson and Mohawk Valley regions. As a result of the dispossession of the Mohawks from their homes and land, white citizens asked Gansevoort if the vacant properties could be turned over to those who had lost their own homes and land in the raids carried out by the British and their Iroquois allies. This action, however, was condemned by Philip Schuyler because many of the Mohawks of the Teantontalago region had supported the Americans in their cause.

SULLIVAN'S CAMPAIGN WAS SUCCESSFUL in that Sullivan's army was able to destroy more than forty Iroquois villages and an assortment of individuals homes outside of the villages, as well as over 160,000 bushels of corn and a large number of other vegetables and fruit. They were able to accomplish this with the loss of only forty lives; however, the Sullivan Campaign failed in its objective to capture Native American prisoners. The implications of the Sullivan Campaign were the destruction of villages and homes as well as food stores and supplies belonging to the various Native groups in the affected areas; however, another major implication of the Sullivan Campaign was that Native tribes who were neutral or had harbored Patriot sympathies would turn to the British for protection from the American attacks on their lands and the pillaging of their food and supplies. If the Americans had hoped to garner the support of many of New York's Native peoples, they had lost the opportunity to do so with the actions of the Sullivan Campaign.

The Sullivan Campaign had a number of social implications that are worth mentioning, including the increase in American morale at its successful conclusion. The Sullivan Campaign achieved its goals of the destruction of Iroquois villages, food and supplies that could be used to benefit the British army while the American Revolution was still underway. Other social implications include the loss of morale for the Iroquois and their loss of support for the British army. Due to his reputation during the French and Indian War, General George Washington had earned the nickname "Town Destroyer" among the Seneca, and this nickname would stick with him as a result of the Sullivan Campaign and his role in assigning the generals to head the campaign with the goal of the destruction of Mohawk and Seneca villages.

The irony of the Sullivan Campaign was that the campaign itself was viewed as a retaliatory method by the Americans for the destruction of towns and villages in New York and Pennsylvania by Brant's forces and the forces of other British commanding officers, but the British and Iroquois forces viewed those actions as necessary because they believed that the Americans would go after the Iroquois and destroy their villages after the American success at the Battle of Saratoga. Both sides involved in the raids in the second half of the 1770s believed they were doing the right thing for their people and that their actions were protective and on the defensive.

Although not a major British action against the people of New York during the Revolution, the Sullivan Campaign does highlight that the raids perpetuated by the Loyalists and their Iroquois allies did not go unchecked during the war. The fear that New Yorkers felt for the unpredictable British and Iroquois raids were justified, and the Patriot-leaning New Yorkers did what they felt was right by going to the Continental army so they might bring an end to the raids.

10

DISPOSSESSING NEW YORK
LOYALISTS

The American Revolution would come to an end in 1783, with the surrender of British general Horatio Gates to American general George Washington in Yorktown, Virginia. With the end of the war came the end of the British raids in New York. The raiding forces disbanded at the end of the following year, and the former Loyalists would struggle after the disbanding of the troops. Many would leave the states and make lives for themselves in Upper Canada, and some would move across the pond to Britain, while others would continue to live in their home states. What the bulk of these former Loyalists experienced after the end of the war was not a happy beginning in a new nation but instead the action of being dispossessed of their property and banished from their home states.

During the American Revolution, many states passed a series of laws that allowed them to seize the property belonging to known Loyalists. These confiscation laws criminalized dissent against the Revolution, punishing those who chose the "wrong side." These confiscation laws also served as a means of banishing known Loyalists from New York State if they had not left the state voluntarily, as many had done both during and after the Revolution. For example, the Jessup brothers of Upstate New York had fled to Canada before the Revolution came to an end. The over one million acres of land they owned in modern-day Warren County was forfeited to the State of New York and became the towns of Lake Luzerne, Corinth, Warrensburg, Thurman, Chestertown and Johnstown. Per the confiscation laws, the properties would either be sold for profit or redistributed to the

Cannoneers at Fort William Henry in Lake George, New York. The fort was burned down by the French and their Native American allies in the 1750s but was replaced with nearby Fort George, which was raided by the British and their Iroquois allies in the later 1770s during the American Revolution. *Wikimedia Commons.*

British soldiers in battle. *Wikimedia Commons.*

Left: Fife and drum corps. *Marie D.A. Williams.*

Below: The past and present collide as reenactors and park visitors discuss the American Revolution at the Saratoga National Battlefield Park. *Marie D.A. Williams.*

community. New York, at this time, built one of the strongest property seizure actions, and the act of depriving some people of their property would become legitimized.

The act of seizing Loyalist properties and either auctioning off or redistributing the lands began as early as 1777, with the most aggressive of these confiscation laws being passed in October 1779. This act, referred to as the Forfeiture Act, included a list of New York Loyalists, both prominent and little-known, and stated that the individuals who were listed had forfeited their property, had forfeited their right to own property in the state and were banished from living in the state. The state had been given the power the sell the forfeited property for profit.

A Revolutionary-era surgeon's kit. *Marie D.A. Williams.*

Right: An officer discusses horse care on the battlefield. *Marie D.A. Williams.*

Below: An American camp follower lays out the washing to dry in the sun. *Marie D.A. Williams.*

Soldiers preparing for battle. *Marie D.A. Williams.*

Camp followers' belongings under a tree. *Marie D.A. Williams.*

A soldier's coat dries in the sun on a cannon. *Marie D.A. Williams.*

British camp followers mending clothing and chatting. *Marie D.A. Williams.*

British soldiers overlooking the battlefield. *Marie D.A. Williams.*

A soldier's gear and weapons. *Marie D.A. Williams.*

Similar laws in the very early 1800s would get the public involved in the process of property seizure. If a New Yorker were to prove to the surveyor general that there was unsold property that belonged to once treasonous individuals, the person who brought the property to the attention of the surveyor general would be granted 25 percent of the total property value once the land was sold.

As can be imagined, individuals would fight against the forfeiture and confiscation acts, taking the matter to the courts. A young New York lawyer named Alexander Hamilton, later the first secretary of the treasury of the United States, is credited with helping former Loyalists reclaim their seized property. The reasoning behind Hamilton's assistance was that many of the former Loyalists were very wealthy, and he believed that if they were to reclaim their property and live in the new United States, their wealth could help bolster the economy. Hamilton believed that instead of banishing former Loyalists, they could be reintegrated into the new American society, and at least at some level, the former Loyalists who chose to stay in New York were able to successfully become part of the new nation.

AFTERWORD

The raids that were carried out in New York greatly affected the people who resided in the state regardless of which side of the conflict they were on. For the British, these raids were seen as a means to prevent the Americans from gathering the supplies they needed to become a major fighting force. For the Americans, the raids were seen as retaliation for the British-led raids. New York was seen as a strategic area at the time of the American Revolution, and the unsuccessful three-pronged campaign carried out by the British to capture the Hudson and Mohawk Rivers and cut the thirteen colonies in two was a major blow to the British.

The resulting raids carried out by the British and their Iroquois allies came at a high cost for those who resided in the areas. Families were forced to leave their homes due to the destruction of their houses and farmland; families were torn apart by death and captivity; the Iroquois were divided—some wanted to remain neutral while others wanted to fight for either side of the Revolution; people left New York for Canada, only to join up with the British and carry out raids themselves; and other people did what they could to supply the American forces with food and goods while defending their homes and livelihoods. The Hudson and Mohawk River Valleys were pillaged and plundered at the time of the war. The people, regardless of which side they chose to support, endured so much. However, in 1783, when the war had ended, George Washington visited the areas that were once torn apart by the raids, and he saw fields of wheat and farmers and their families returning to the land. After the Revolution and the series of raids in the areas had come to an end, the areas of the Hudson River Valley and the Mohawk River Valley would become peaceful areas.

The history of one's home state is a history that should not be ignored, no matter how uncomfortable it may seem, and everyone deserves to have their story told. It is a history that can make connections between what one already knows about oneself and about the country as a whole. Historian David C. McCullough said, "History is who we are and why we are the way we are. History is not just the past. History is the present," and this is true beyond a shadow of a doubt.

In the first half of the American Revolution, New Yorkers, particularly those who resided in Upstate New York, were either Loyalists or were indifferent toward either side and did not view the war as something with which they should concern themselves. The Saratoga Campaign and the raids perpetrated by the British after their failure at the Battle of Saratoga would change the minds of Upstate New Yorkers. There was a notable increase in numbers for the American military forces at the battle's conclusion, and many sought to protect their homes and livelihoods from the British forces should they retaliate for the loss, which they did through the series of raids described in this narrative. However, many New Yorkers also joined with the British during the years of the raids, believing that they and their property would be safe from harm.

Throughout the process of researching and writing this book, there was a series of questions in the back of my mind: To what extent is history a search for truth? What can we know about the past? Why is history worth studying? Why am I choosing to write about these raids? I'd like to take the time to address these questions now in a way I could not do throughout the historical narrative presented in this book.

The last question in this series is the easiest of these to answer. I chose to focus my research on the British raids in New York because the raids are largely unknown. Until I was researching these raids for my graduate thesis, I did not know that the town where I went to school as a child and adolescent had once been owned by Loyalists or that the British twice burned down the town where my husband works, and I could guarantee that others had not heard of these events either. I wanted to share my newly acquired knowledge with as many people as I could, and I wanted to delve deeper into these events and thought this was the best way to accomplish both of those tasks.

The remaining three questions all take quite a bit more thought to answer.

To what extent is history a search for truth? I believe that we can never truly know everything about the past, but that does not mean we should not pursue the answers to questions we have about the past. At its core, history is a search for truth. Those who choose to dedicate themselves to the study of history are searching for the answers to an endless number of questions. For me, the question that inspired the research for this historical narrative was, "What were the Loyalists doing in New York after the Saratoga Campaign?" In school, while learning about the American Revolution, there was a major focus on the American Patriots but not on their Loyalist counterparts. I, and historians much more seasoned than myself, sought out the truth to answer this burning question. Historians are always searching for the truth—they are the fact checkers of the past, digging through archives that have not seen the light of day in decades, and their research often does not receive the recognition it deserves.

The next question, "What can we know about the past?" is one without a specific answer. As long as people inquire about the past, as long as there are people who keep searching for answers to those questions, as long as there are people willing to share those results, we have the opportunity to know an immeasurable amount of information about the past.

This final question, "Why is history worth studying?" is a question I have been asked more times than I can count from everyone who wanted to know why I decided to become a history teacher and independent historian. Each historian may have their own answer to this question based on their specific area of focus in history. For me, history is worth studying because it can teach us the good, bad and neutral things in which our nation has been involved. It can teach us about the lives of prominent figures, innovative inventions and plans gone awry and so much more. History is also worth studying because the past can have a major effect on the present, especially when it comes to politics and economics. Finally, history is worth studying because the subject is one that can help build well-rounded individuals by keeping them informed on the past events, politics, economics, literature, advances in the STEM fields and more.

The history of New York State is a topic that has interested me since I was a child, and I am so grateful to The History Press for the opportunity to contribute to its vast historiography.

Appendix

TIMELINES BY CHAPTER

Chapter 1

July 5, 1777: Americans evacuate Fort Ticonderoga.

July 7, 1777: Battle of Hubbardton (colonial New Hampshire/modern-day Vermont); no clear victory for either side.

July 8, 1777: British victory at the Battle of Fort Anne.

July 27, 1777: Murder of Jane McCrea, a young Loyalist woman.

July 29, 1777: British forces take Fort Edward and Fort George.

August 6, 1777: British defeat at the Battle of Oriskany.

August 15, 1777: British defeat at the Battle of Bennington.

September 19, 1777: British victory at the Battle of Freeman's Farm, the first of the two encounters at Saratoga.

September 20–October 7, 1777: British defeat at the Battle of Bemis Heights, the second of the two encounters at Saratoga.

Chapter 4

May 10, 1775: American capture of Fort Ticonderoga by Colonel Benedict Arnold and Ethan Allen.

September 17–November 3, 1775: American victory at the Siege of Fort St. Jean; Province of Quebec, Upper Canada.

December 30–31, 1775: British victory at the Battle of Quebec.

October 11, 1776: British tactical victory at the Battle of Valcour Island.

1782: Sir Guy Carleton takes over as the commander-in-chief of the British forces in North America.
August 1783: Carleton oversees the evacuation of British forces from New York City.
1786: Carleton becomes governor of Quebec, Nova Scotia and New Brunswick.

Chapter 5

1749: Christopher Carleton, nephew of Sir Guy Carleton, born in Newcastle upon Tyne, England.
May 1776: Captain Christopher Carleton is called to Quebec City as part of a relief force during the Battle of Quebec.
October 11, 1776: British tactical victory at the Battle of Valcour Island.
October 6, 1778: Forces under Captain Carleton are successful in raiding the Fort Ticonderoga area for supplies and cattle.
October 10–11, 1780: Christopher Carleton, now a major, leads a raiding expedition against Fort Anne, Fort George, Kingsbury, Queensbury, Glens Falls, Fort Edward and Fort Miller.
October 11–12, 1780: British raid on Ball's Town (modern-day Ballston Spa, near Saratoga).

Chapter 6

Mid-1760s: Brothers Edward and Ebenezer Jessup move from Dutchess County, New York, to Albany, New York, to participate in land speculation.
1760s–1775: The Jessups become associated with Sir William Johnson and the Mohawk Nation and purchase large tracts of land that become the towns of Lake Luzerne, Corinth, Hadley, Warrensburg, Thurman, Chestertown and Johnsburg.
1763: Edward and Ebenezer begin lumbering operations in what would become the town of Lake Luzerne and Corinth.
Winter 1775: Colonists begin destroying property belonging to the Jessups—burning the mills, destroying a ferry and even ransacking the Jessup homestead.
Summer 1776: Edward and Ebenezer Jessup lead a party of eighty Loyalist troops to Crown Point to aid the British forces stationed there.

May 6, 1777: Thirty-one Loyalists are captured on or near the Jessup Patent. Edward Jessup flees, following along the Hudson River, to meet his brother and General John Burgoyne encamped at Willsborough Falls.

Summer–October 1777: The Jessup brothers participate in Burgoyne's Saratoga Campaign, even taking part in Burgoyne's surrender at Saratoga in October.

October 1778: Ebenezer Jessup participates in Christopher Carleton's series of raids in the Hudson Valley region.

November 1781: Edward Jessup named major commandant of a new corps of Loyal Rangers, known as Jessup's Rangers.

November 1781–spring 1783: Edward Jessup and his Jessup's Rangers participate in a series of raids of small towns and settlements bordering the Jessup Patent, including raids against Queensbury, Glens Falls, Kingsbury, Fort Edward and Fort Anne.

Mid- to late 1780s: The Jessup brothers settle in upper Canada after the American victory concluding the American Revolution.

1785–February 1816: Edward Jessup continues his land speculating and establishs the town of Prescott in upper Canada. Edward passes away in February 1816.

Chapter 7

May 21, 1780: Sir John Johnson, son of Sir William Johnson, carries out his first raid on the Mohawk Valley region, attacking Johnstown and Caughnawaga (modern-day Fonda).

October 12, 1780: Sir John Johnson carries out his second raid on the Mohawk Valley region, attacking Schoharie, Middleburg and Fort Hunter.

October 19, 1780: Sir John Johnson participates in the Battle of Stone Arabia and Battle of Klock's Field (modern-day St. Johnsville), resulting in a victory for the British.

Chapter 8

May 30, 1778: Joseph Brant raids Cobleskill.

September 17, 1778: Joseph Brant raids German Flatts.

October 8, 1778: Joseph Brant raids Ulster County while Walter Butler raids Onaquaga and Unadilla.

November 11, 1778: Joseph Brant and Walter Butler raid Cherry Valley.

April 7, 1780: Joseph Brant attacks American rebels at Harpersfield in the Schoharie Valley.

July 24, 1780: Joseph Brant raids and burns the Oneida village of Canowaraghere near Fort Stanwix in Oriskany.

July 26, 1780: Joseph Brant attacks the Oneida Natives who fled to Fort Stanwix.

August 2, 1780: Joseph Brant attacks Canajoharie and Fort Plain.

August 9, 1780: Joseph Brant attacks Vroomans near Middle Fort in modern-day Middleburg.

October 19, 1780: Brant participates in Sir John Johnson's attack on Stone Arabia and Klock's Field.

Summer 1783: Brant initiates the formation of the ill-fated Western Confederacy.

CHAPTER NINE

July–August 1779: The American forces under General John Sullivan encamp at Tioga on the New York–Pennsylvania border, awaiting men and supplies that were slow to arrive to them.

August 26, 1779: Sullivan's forces leave Tioga and begin their raids in the First Nations territories.

August 29, 1779: American victory at the Battle of Newtown.

September 5, 1779: Americans take the village of Kendaia along the western shore of Seneca Lake.

September 10, 1779: Americans reach Canandaigua.

September 11, 1779: Americans reach Honeoye.

September 13, 1779: An American scouting force is nearly wiped out in an ambush near Geneseo; its leader, a Lieutenant Boyd, is killed during the ambush.

September 14, 1779: Americans reach Geneseo.

September 17, 1779: Americans reach Honeoye a second time.

September 27, 1779: A portion of General Clinton's brigade under the command of Colonel Peter Gansevoort leaves to winter in the vicinity of Fort Stanwix; a detachment of that brigade stops at Teantontalago, where they take the male Mohawk Natives and incarcerate them in Albany, New York, until 1780, when they are released. The Americans, at this time, also dispossess the Mohawk Natives of their land.

September 30, 1779: The end of the Sullivan Campaign.

BIBLIOGRAPHY

"The Battle of Cherry Valley (Massacre)." https://revolutionarywar.us/year-1778/battle-cherry-valley-massacre.

Bennett, David. *A Few Lawless Vagabonds: Ethan Allen, the Republic of Vermont, and the American Revolution.* Philadelphia, PA: Casemate Publishers, 2014.

Boonshoft, Mark. "Dispossessing Loyalists and Redistributing Property in Revolutionary New York." September 19, 2016. www.nypl.org/blog/beta/2016/09/19/loyalist-property-confiscation.

Breen, T.H. *American Insurgents, American Patriots: The Revolution of the People.* New York: Hill and Wang, 2010.

Campbell, William W. *The Annals of Tryon County, or The Border Warfare of New York During the Revolution.* New York: J & J Harper, 1831.

Countryman, Edward. *A People in Revolution: The American Revolution and Political Society in New York, 1760–1790.* New York: Johns Hopkins University Press, 1981.

Fort Stanwix National Monument Staff. "The Clinton-Sullivan Campaign of 1779." https://www.nps.gov/fost/learn/historyculture/the-western-expedition-against-the-six-nations-1779.htm.

Glidden, G. William. "The Jessups, Adirondack Land Barons." Warren County Historical Society. February 1, 2015. http://www.warrencountyhistoricalsociety.org/publications/rewind-october-15-2017-abraham-lincoln-and-upstate-new-york/rewind-2015/rewind-february-1-2015-the-jessups-adirondack-land-barons.

History.com Staff. "Poor Leadership Leads to Cherry Valley Massacre." November 11, 2009. https://www.history.com/this-day-in-history/poor-leadership-leads-to-cherry-valley-massacre.

Kelsay, Isabel Thompson. *Joseph Brant: A Man of Two Worlds, 1743–1807.* Syracuse, NY: Syracuse University Press, 1984.

Logusz, Michael O. *With Musket and Tomahawk: The Mohawk Valley Campaign in the Wilderness War of 1777.* Havertown, PA: Casemate Publishers, 2012.

———. *With Musket and Tomahawk: The Saratoga Campaign in the Wilderness War of 1777.* Havertown, PA: Casemate, 2010.

Lowenthal, Larry, ed. *Days of Siege: A Journal of the Siege of Fort Stanwix.* New York: Eastern Acorn Press, 1983.

Mohawk Valley Region. "American Revolution in the Mohawk Valley Region." Path Through History. https://www.mohawkvalleyhistory.com/themes/revolutionary-war.

Native Heritage Project. "Nicholas Cusick—Revolutionary War Patriot, Sachem, Tuscarora Chief." May 2, 2012. https://nativeheritageproject.com/2012/05/02/nicholas-cusick-revolutionary-war-patriot-sachem-tuscarora-chief.

———. "The Tuscarora and the Revolutionary War." May 28, 2012. https://nativeheritageproject.com/2012/05/28/the-tuscarora-and-the-revolutionary-war.

Oneida Indian Nation. "The Revolutionary War, Oneida's Legacy to Freedom." http://www.oneidaindiannation.com/revolutionarywar.

Saratoga County Chamber of Commerce. "The Battle of Saratoga." https://www.saratoga.org/tourism/battle-of-saratoga.

Sawyer, William. "The 1777 Siege of Fort Schuyler." National Park Service. https://www.nps.gov/fost/learn/historyculture/the-1777-siege-of-fort-schuyler.htm.

Snow, Dean. *1777: Tipping Point at Saratoga.* New York: Oxford University Press, 2016.

Town of Saratoga Historian's Office. "Baroness Described the 1st Battle of Saratoga." September 22, 2016. https://historianatsaratoga.wordpress.com.

Washington, Ida H., and Paul A. Washington. *Carleton's Raid.* Weybridge, VT: Cherry Tree Books, 1977.

Watt, Gavin K. *The Burning of the Valleys: Daring Raids from Canada Against the New York Frontier in the Fall of 1780.* Toronto, ON: Dundurn, 1997.

Wood, Gordon S. *The Radicalism of the American Revolution.* New York: Random House, 1991.

ABOUT THE AUTHOR

Marie Danielle Annette Williams is an independent historian living in Upstate New York. She received her bachelor of arts degree in social studies adolescent education from the College of Saint Rose in Albany, New York, in 2014 and received her master of arts degree in American history from Southern New Hampshire University in Manchester, New Hampshire, in 2018. She has been writing about American history since 2011 on her blog titled *The Half-Pint Historian Blog* and has contributed articles to the *Adirondack Almanack* and the *New York History Blog*.

Visit us at
www.historypress.com
....